Strategies and Rational Decisions
in the Securities Options Market

BURTON G. MALKIEL *and* RICHARD E. QUANDT

Strategies and Rational Decisions in the Securities Options Market

The MIT Press
Cambridge, Massachusetts, and London, England

To our fathers

Contents

Figures

Tables

Preface

This book reports on a practical application of some highly theoretical constructs of economic theory. Those aspects of our work most directly pertinent to the application involve much arcane material characteristically known only to tax lawyers and other Wall Street practitioners. In contrast, only economists are usually privy to the methodology we have adopted. The particular marriage entered into in these pages resulted from our profound interest in the substantive questions concerning optimal investment policy and our thorough conviction that economic theory can contribute to the solution of practical problems.

We feel that this book will be of relevance both to economists, who rarely see concrete applications of utility theory and of the theory of games against nature, and to practical men interested in sound investment strategies.

Not all parts of the book may appeal equally to all men. Although Chapter 1, describing the history of options, will be of interest to all, the details of Chapter 2, dealing with the technical details of options, including some thorny issues of the investor's tax liability, may be of more interest to market practitioners, though much of this institutional detail must be understood to follow the remainder of the book. Chapter 3, concerned with the utility theory underlying our work and the audacity of our economic assumptions, will appeal more to economists. Chapters 4 and 5 deal with the results of our analysis and should appeal to all — particularly to those with concrete and detailed investment problems — although it will be fully understandable only by those with the necessary theoretical background. Chapter 6 presents the most generally valid conclusions in a manner accessible to all types of readers and should be of general interest.

Many more people have helped us with facts and methods than can possibly be remembered accurately. Among economists we are particularly indebted to William J. Baumol who read the entire manuscript and offered several extremely valuable suggestions. We also had helpful comments from Paul Cootner, Alvin Klevorick, Fritz Machlup, Jacob Michaelson, and Hale Trotter. Their suggestions for improving both content and exposition were invaluable. Among those who are active in the investment field we are greatly in debt to Henry Brach, Paul Farmer, Carl Icahn, Henry Kane, David Lederman, Gerard Snyder, and Harold Webb. They helped us with critical comments, provided us with insight into the practical workings of the option market, and gave us an invaluable testing ground for our ideas. Additional useful comments were received from audiences at various seminars where we presented partial results: at The Institute of Management Sciences meetings on April 6, 1967, at the Institute for Quantitative Research in Finance meetings on April 25, 1968, at the University of Pennsylvania, the University of York, and the Massachusetts Institute of Technology. We obtained data through the courtesy of the Securities and Exchange Commission, and the Put and Call Brokers and Dealers Association. Research assistants who helped us in various phases of the work were Alan Blinder, Jeffrey Balash, Raymond Hartman, Robert Lem, and Chester Seabury. The diagrams were prepared by Mrs. Charlotte Carlson. Finally, we wish to express our gratitude to Mrs. Catherine Brown and to Mrs. Helen Talar for typing impeccably several drafts.

We also gratefully acknowledge financial support from the National Science Foundation, the Ford Foundation, and the Institute for Quantitative Research in Finance.

Burton G. Malkiel
Richard E. Quandt
January 31, 1969

Strategies and Rational Decisions in the Securities Options Market

Introduction

A consumer is acting rationally when he apportions his limited income among alternative consumption goods in such a manner as to achieve the highest level of satisfaction that can be attained with that income. Although the theoretical problem of maximizing an index of satisfaction (the utility function) subject to a budget constraint can be formulated and solved quite easily in mathematical terms, in practice economists proceed somewhat differently when they attempt to measure or explain the demand for some commodity. One basic reason for this is that the individual's utility function is not directly observable. But other, equally practical, obstacles prevent a direct approach. Among these is the fact that the full range of potentially consumable commodities, even though perhaps not infinitely large, is still sufficiently extensive to make dealing with a "realistic" utility function impracticable.

A similar problem confronts the individual in his capacity as investor of the funds he has decided not to consume. He may turn such funds into a variety of assets, differing from each other primarily in terms of yield and risk. In principle, we can again formulate the problem of optimal or rational action as one of utility maximization: the investor should so allocate his funds among alternative assets as to maximize some measure of total satisfaction.

Such a general formulation is again not a practical procedure when we wish to solve the concrete problem of rational action for the individual investor who wishes to allocate his savings among alternative assets. Practically useful procedures are simpler and more straightforward. There are at least two approaches to the determination of rational or optimal investment strategies.

The first, and conceptually perhaps the simplest approach,

consists of determining the expected value of some particular set of investment strategies, such as buying common stock X, buying bond Y, etc.[1] The expected monetary value of an investment is the relevant criterion for the investor only if he is neutral with respect to risk, i.e., if he has no preference for one type of asset over another when they both have the same expected value but differ in their degrees of risk. If this assumption of risk neutrality is not justified, we must explicitly introduce the investor's utility function and deal not with the expected monetary value but the expected utility of the security in question. Whichever is the case, if such evaluations were made, the individual would select the investment that gives him the most favorable expected utility, given his attitude toward risk. Characteristically, this type of approach deals with investments of the same *type* and considers choice among *different securities*.

A second and more sophisticated approach to this problem consists of the recognition that the choice of an optimal portfolio cannot be made without determining the interrelationships among different securities. Since returns from many types of stocks may tend to move systematically in similar or opposite directions, we must now take into account not only the expected return and the variance (i.e., risk) but also the covariance of returns.[2]

In contrast to these approaches, our own analysis deals with a single hypothetical stock and examines the consequences to the investor of many different *types* of investments involving that stock. As such, it does not purport to answer questions of optimal portfolio composition of the Markowitz type. It is rather based on the fact that the decision to "do something with stock X" does not automatically mean that the investor should buy the shares. Perhaps he should buy the shares on margin, or sell them short, or buy or sell some type of option on them. Our analysis is thus mainly concerned with the determination of optimal *types* of investment strategies.

It is to be expected that the optimal types of strategies will de-

---

[1] Clearly, this may be more easily said than done, since the proposed procedure requires as a minimum some insight into the probability distribution of the relevant stock or bond price changes over the period of time for which the investment is contemplated. At this introductory stage we say nothing about how those questions may be answered.

[2] See Harry Markowitz, *Portfolio Selection* (New York: Wiley, 1959).

pend on both the characteristics of the stock in question and on the characteristics of the individual investor. In order to guard ourselves against reaching conclusions in too facile a manner, we have examined the consequences of each of a large variety of hypothetical stocks combined with each of a large variety of hypothetical investors. We have examined volatile stocks and stocks with relatively stable prices, and stocks paying or not paying dividends. We have examined investors who are bullish or bearish with respect to future prices, and investors who are aggressive or conservative with respect to their relative evaluation of the satisfaction derived from gains and losses. Altogether, we have examined the consequences of 1056 distinct combinations of assumptions about the stock and the investor. The details of the various assumptions are discussed in Chapters 2 and 3, and the analysis of results is contained in Chapters 4 and 5.

Of course, the conclusions ought to be believed only to the extent that the underlying assumptions are plausible. Some of our conclusions, such as the major one that employing investment strategies involving stock options is very much more profitable than is often believed, are firmly established because they appear to hold irrespective of what we assume about the characteristics of the stock and the investors. Others, such as the conclusion that tax-exempt and conservative institutions can derive substantially improved portfolio performance from writing Call options or Straddles against their portfolio, are more restricted in their applicability. It is the task of Chapter 6 to pull together the detailed analyses of Chapters 4 and 5 and to discuss those conclusions that are most interesting and widely applicable.

The generalized portfolio problem is still an open one. In a realistic context the investor's problem is neither to select a combination of stocks that he will buy nor to select the appropriate type of investment strategy for a given stock, but to solve those problems jointly: for all possible stocks and all possible investment strategies that can be undertaken with respect to any one stock, he must decide on the optimal combination of stocks and investment strategies. The solution of this general problem promises to be a very difficult one. Our hope is that we have contributed to the solution of one important part of it successfully.

CHAPTER ONE

Security Options: Historical Background and Present Organization of the Market

The market for Put and Call options on equity securities is a relatively little understood yet an increasingly important modern financial institution. Options have had a long and somewhat checkered history. They were widely used during the tulip-bulb craze in Holland in the seventeenth century, and ever since they have been attacked by public officials as an instrument of unhealthy speculation. Because of their association with speculative excesses, they were banned outright in England on different occasions. Perhaps their reputation at various times as the "black sheep" of the securities field may explain the fact that they have received relatively little attention from either the financial or academic communities. We hope that this study will help both to increase our understanding of stock options and to assess their role in the general context of security trading.

In this chapter we first describe the basic option types and present a brief historical survey of option dealing. Then the current organization of the market is described, and the theoretical and empirical literature on option trading is reviewed. Next, the results of a cross-sectional study of the determination of option premiums is presented. Finally, against this background, the focus of the present study is explained.

1.1
The Basic Option Types

Although a thorough analysis of the basic option strategies will be deferred until the next chapter, it will be useful at the outset to present a brief description of security options here. A Call option is an option to buy a specified number of shares (usually 100), at any time within the contract period, at a stated price (the option price), which is usually the market price at the time the option is written. The option price is reduced for any dividends paid during the life of the option and, as thus reduced, the option price is called the "striking price." A Put option gives the holder the right to sell a specified number of shares at a fixed price at any time within the contract period. These options are sold (issued) by individuals or financial institutions for a cash consideration called the option premium. The sellers (or writers) of Call options take on the obligation to deliver the shares at the contract price if and when the option holder chooses to "call" them from him. The seller of the Put contract is obliged to buy the shares at the striking price if the option buyer wishes to "put" the shares to him. Whether or not the options are exercised depends, of course, on the movements of the market price of the shares after the option is sold.

Puts and Calls are the basic option contracts. Certain combinations of these options and variations in contract terms are also often used. A Straddle is a combination of one Put and one Call option. The buyer of a Straddle has the right either to buy the stock from or sell it to the seller of the contract at the striking price during the period of the option's validity. The exercise of one part of the Straddle contract does not invalidate the other part. Similar to the Straddle but far less popular is the Spread, consisting of a simultaneous Put and Call option where the option prices for the two contracts are not the same. The option price for the Put is usually below the market price when the option is written while the Call price is typically above the market price. A Strip is a combination option consisting of two Puts and one Call, while a Strap consists of two Calls and one Put.

1.2
The Historical Background of Option Dealings

Options have had a long and not always respectable past. According to one interpreter, the earliest reference to a business option appears in *The Bible*.[1] The incident occurred when Jacob wished to

---

[1] Genesis 29. See **Anthony M. Reinach**, *The Nature of Puts and Calls* (New York: The Bookmailer, 1961) p. 32.

marry Rachel, youngest daughter of Laban. Laban agreed, provided that Jacob would first pay him seven years of labor. After that period Jacob would have an option on Rachel's hand. If this transaction was indeed an option,[2] we can see how options were already off to a bad start since Laban reneged on the contract and gave Jacob his elder daughter, Leah, instead.

Aristotle reported in his *Politics* that the ancient philosopher Thales amassed a fortune through options.[3] "Seeing in the stars" that next year's olive crop would be an exceptionally large one, Thales took options on the use of virtually all the olive presses in Miletus for the next harvest season. By "leveraging" his capital in this way, he achieved a corner on the presses, and then, when the bumper crop came in, he was able to lease them back at exorbitant rates.

Options made their first major mark on economic history during the legendary tulip-bulb craze in seventeenth-century Holland. Although tulip bulbs had been introduced from Turkey a century before, during the 1630's the Dutch became so enchanted with them that their prices began to rise wildly. Reinach reports that "Tulip-bulb trading seemed so lucrative that rich and poor alike abandoned the ordinary industry of the country to embark upon this trade."[4] Options first were used in this situation for hedging. For example, by purchasing a Call a dealer who was committed to a sales contract could assure himself that he could obtain a fixed number of bulbs for a set price on a specific day. Similarly, tulip-bulb growers could assure themselves of selling their bulbs at a set price by purchasing Put options. Later, however, options were increasingly employed by speculators who found that Call options were an effective vehicle for obtaining maximum possible gains per dollar of investment. As long as prices continued to skyrocket, Call buyers realized returns far in

---

[2] Benton E. Gup has argued that it is inappropriate to regard this transaction as an option. An essential element of all early Hebrew marriages was the payment of a sum (the Mohar) by the bridegroom to the father of the bride. Payment for the bride by serivce, as in Jacob's case, was not uncommon. See Benton E. Gup, "The Economics of the Security Option Markets," unpublished Ph.D. dissertation, University of Cincinnati, 1966, pp. 14–15.

[3] Henry C. Emery, "Speculation on the Stock and Produce Exchanges of the United States," in *Studies in History, Economics and Public Law* VII (New York: Columbia University, 1896) p. 315.

[4] Reinach, *Puts and Calls*, p. 33.

excess of those obtained by speculators who purchased tulip bulbs themselves. The writers of Put options also prospered as bulb prices spiraled.

The inevitable break in the market occurred in 1636. As prices plummeted, thousands of investors whose life savings were invested in tulip bulbs went bankrupt. Hardest hit were the Put writers who were unable to meet their commitments. A prolonged economic depression ensued in Holland. As a result of the collapse and the involvement of Puts and Calls in the preceding speculative mania, options acquired a bad name, which they have retained more or less to the present time.

Apparently, there was a well organized and rather sophisticated market in Puts and Calls in London during the 1690's.[5] From the very beginning, however, considerable opposition developed to the use of stock options because of their association with excessive speculation. They were declared illegal by Barnard's Act of 1733 and were regarded as being disreputable by the major brokerage houses.[6] The act was ineffective, however, in stopping option dealings.

In 1821, while Barnard's Act was still in effect, the controversy over stock options almost precipitated a split in the London Stock Exchange.[7] When the Stock Exchange Committee proposed a rule forbidding members of the Exchange from dealing in options (which were illegal anyway) "a large number of members rose in arms against the innovation." [8] The dissident group went so far as to raise the money for a rival stock exchange building. Finally, the matter was dropped and option trading continued. Barnard's Act itself was repealed in 1860.

Option dealings continued throughout the nineteenth century in England but on a reduced scale, since many prominent firms refused to take part in them. In our century options were banned during the financial crisis of 1931 and for an extended period between World War II and 1958.[9] Members of the Labour party tended

---

[5] E. Victor Morgan, and W. A. Thomas, *The Stock Exchange* (London: Elek Books, 1962) p. 21.

[6] *Ibid.*, p. 61.

[7] Charles Duguid, *The Story of the Stock Exchange* (London: Grant Richards, 1901) pp. 121–122.

[8] *Ibid.*, p. 122.

[9] Morgan and Thomas, *Stock Exchange*, pp. 219, 224, 236.

to be particularly critical of security options, regarding them as evidence that the stock exchange was merely a den of gamblers. Since 1958 only five firms have acted as option dealers, and the volume of transactions has been considerably smaller than during the prewar period when, despite all the opposition to options, London was the most important option market in the world.[10]

As in Britain, options have also had a controversial history in the United States. The first mention of options in American history dates back to 1790 about a century after their debut in England.[11] Option and futures trading flourished during the Civil War and its aftermath.[12] As the progressive movement swept the country, however, all sorts of speculation fell into disfavor. In the late nineteenth century options on commodity exchanges were regarded as gambling contracts and hence illegal and unenforceable.[13] Stock options were never banned, however, despite several attempts around the turn of the century to abolish them as part of a general program against dishonesty and speculation.

Interest in stock options increased considerably during the bull markets of the 1920's.[14] Unfortunately, the most flagrant abuse of

---

[10] Option markets also exist in France, West Germany, and Switzerland, but, as in the case of the United Kingdom, many of these markets have declined considerably. See G. Krefetz and R. Marossi, *Investing Abroad* (New York: Harper and Row, 1965), pp. 47, 141, and Hesslein, "Puts and Calls," Memorandum Presented to the SEC, 1934. Unlike the option contracts in the United States, European options cannot be exercised before their expiration date.

[11] Joseph S. Davis, *Essays in the Earlier History of American Corporations* (Cambridge: Harvard University Press, 1917) p. 196.

[12] See Gup, "Security Option Markets," pp. 17–22 and Emery, "Speculation on Stock and Produce Exchanges," pp. 322ff., Gup recounts (p. 21) that many of the better known speculators of the last half of the nineteenth century made use of options in connection with stock transactions and financial in-fighting. Commodore Vanderbilt, Daniel Drew, Jay Gould, and Jim Fisk are some of the names involved. See also Henry Clews, *Twenty-Eight Years in Wall Street* (New York: Irving Publishing Co., 1888) pp. 107–111.

[13] See C. B. Cowing, *Populists, Plungers, and Progressives* (Princeton: Princeton University Press, 1965), p. 15. In theory, the difference between an option and a futures contract, which was legal and enforceable, was that a simple option could be settled in cash, whereas the purchaser of a futures contract would demand delivery of the actual product. In practice the distinction was meaningless because futures contracts were typically settled just as simple options were, that is, in cash.

[14] Trading in those days was largely in two- and three-day Calls. There was even a one-day Call known as a "seven-cigar Call," because it sold for one dollar's worth of stogies. The late Herbert Filer, president of one of the largest option firms and a leading spokesman for the industry, recalled "The idea was to buy one

stock options in the United States occurred during the same period. In 1932 and 1933 a Congressional investigation found that many of the financial abuses in the 1920's were related to the use of options.[15] Through the medium of stock options, manipulators were enabled to carry on large-scale operations with a minimum of financial risk. The *modus operandi* of the manipulators usually involved the formation of a "pool." Large stockholders of a corporation, wishing to increase the market value of their shares, would grant, without cost, options at the current market price on part of their shareholdings to the members of the pool. The pool would attempt to make these options profitable by manipulating the price of the shares. This was usually accomplished by such devices as issuing false and misleading reports about the company, and undertaking simultaneous purchases and sales of shares among the pool members ("wash" sales) to increase market activity, thereby lending support to the rumors of exciting developments in the offing. If they were successful in engineering increased public interest in the shares and higher market values for the security, the pool could then exercise the options at the contract price and sell the called shares on the open market.[16]

As a result of such practices, there was growing Congressional and public concern about stock options. In 1929 the New York Stock Exchange required its members to publicize their dealings in options as part of a program of reform. In 1932 a proposed ban on the trading of options was endorsed by a House committee.[17] During the same year the Senate Committee on Banking and Currency, led by counsel Ferdinand Pecora, probed deeply into general stock exchange practices and the role of stock options in particular. The size

of those 'seven-cigar Calls' and about noon the next day, if the stock had had a run, to sell it for $25 or more — just for the rest of the day. I saw one of my colleagues make $1,200 on a Call like that." See Herbert Filer, *Understanding Put and Call Options* (New York: Crown Publishers, 1959) p. 80.

[15] See U. S. Congress, Senate, Senate Report 1455, *Stock Exchange Practices,* 73rd Cong. 2d sess., 1934, pp. 37–41; C. B. Franklin and M. R. Colberg, "Puts and Calls — A Factual Survey," *J. of Finance* (March 1958), p. 29; and the report of The Twentieth Century Fund, *The Security Markets* (New York, 1935), p. 451.

[16] The writers of the option would also gain through the increased market value of their remaining shares. Options were also frequently issued by officers and directors of companies and these were subject to similar abuses. See Report 1455, *Stock Exchange Practices,* pp. 51–113; and the report of The Twentieth Century Fund, p. 453.

[17] Cowing, *Populists, Plungers, and Progressives,* p. 202.

11

of some of the option contracts during the 1929–1933 period is staggering by present standards. The Committee discovered that there were 286 options written that involved 10,000 shares or more. The total number of shares involved was 17,380,478.[18] This may be contrasted with a survey made during January 1959, which showed that there were only four option contracts written on more than 1000 shares, the largest of which involved only 2600 shares.[19] Another practice uncovered by the investigators of the 1930's consisted of granting Call options to customers' men in brokerage houses as an incentive to "push" a certain issue of stock. The Twentieth Century Fund reported: "According to reliable information, a fairly uniform rate of payment to customers' men has grown to be the custom — a Call on one share of stock for every three he was expected to be able to induce his clients to buy." [20]

By 1934, following President Roosevelt's message to Congress of February 9 asking for legislation to regulate the stock exchange, the movement against stock options became even more intense. The Fletcher-Rayburn bill called for an outright ban on all stock options. Represented by Herbert Filer, the Put and Call brokers, whose very existence was threatened by the measures, protested vigorously, stressing the hedging uses of options and the beneficial functions these instruments served. The option dealers prevailed, and the Securities Act of 1934 did not forbid the use of options although the Securities and Exchange Commission was empowered to regulate them.[21]

In response to the Congressional hearings of 1934, the Put and Call Brokers and Dealers Association (PCBDA) was formed to represent the option dealers. Today, it is a highly organized self-policing organization, and most firms that deal in stock options belong to it. The Association has consistently been willing to adopt recommendations from the SEC staff, and thus direct government regulation has been averted.

---

[18] Senate Report 1455, *Stock Exchange Practices*, p. 45.

[19] Securities and Exchange Commission, *Report on Put and Call Options* (Washington: Government Printing Office, 1961) p. 33.

[20] Report of The Twentieth Century Fund, p. 474.

[21] See Section 9b of the Securities Act of 1934.

1.3

Recent Organization of the Option Market in the United States

After the formation of PCBDA the volume of options traded remained relatively small throughout the 1940's. Beginning with the long bull market in 1950, however, the total sales of Puts and Calls increased considerably. Table 1-1 indicates that between 1950 and

Table 1-1

Volume of Puts and Calls Sold and Relation to Total Volume on the NYSE, 1937–1968[1]

	Volume of Options Sold			Ratio of Total Option Volume to NYSE Reported Volume (per cent)
	All Options	Puts	Calls	
	(shares in thousands)			
1937	2,246	754	1,492	.55
1940	1,205	459	746	.58
1945	2,108	801	1,307	.56
1950	2,631	1,064	1,567	.50
1955	6,012	2,246	3,766	.93
1960	8,561	3,133	5,428	1.12
1965	15,256	4,873	10,383	.98
1968	30,286	8,187	22,099	1.03

SOURCE: Securities and Exchange Commission, *Report on Put and Call Options,* p. 20, unpublished data made available by the Securities and Exchange Commission; and David Lederman, "Put and Call Options with Special Emphasis on Option Portfolios," dissertation submitted to the Graduate School of Business of Stanford University, 1969, p. 43.

[1] Based on reports from Put and Call Brokers and Dealers Association. These data include only sales of original options by writers and do not include sales by one dealer to another.

1968 total sales of Puts and Calls grew from 0.50 per cent of New York Stock Exchange volume to 1.03 per cent. This table probably understates the growing importance of options since there has also been a significant increase in the duration of option contracts sold. Table 1-2 shows the maturity composition of options sold for selected years since 1938.[22]

[22] Option dealers currently estimate that on particularly active days option sales amount to as much as 3 per cent of the total New York Stock Exchange volume.

Table 1-2

Volume of Options Sold Classified by
Duration of Option Contract 1938–1965
(shares in thousands)

Year	Total	30–Day Options		60– and 90–Day Options		Over 90–Day Options	
		Shares	Per Cent	Shares	Per Cent	Shares	Per Cent
1938			85.2[1]		14.8		None
1940			63.1[1]		36.9		None
1945	2,108	438	20.8	1,111	52.7	559	26.5
1950	2,631	248	9.4	1,282	48.7	1,101	41.8
1955	6,012	310	5.2	2,860	47.6	2,842	47.3
1960	8,561	320	3.7	2,607	30.5	5,634	65.8
1965	15,256	820	5.4	5,305	34.8	9,131	59.9

SOURCE: 1938–1940: C. B. Franklin and M. R. Colberg, "Puts and Calls: A Factual Survey," *J. of Finance* (March 1958), p. 27.
1945–1960: Securities and Exchange Commission, *Report on Put and Call Options,* p. 24.
1965: Unpublished data made available by the Securities and Exchange Commission.
[1] Includes options maturing in under 30 days.

During the 1930's the majority of options were written for 30 days or less, with 7-day options comprising a significant share of the total. The very short options declined in importance during the early 1940's and in 1945 the PCBDA prohibited dealings in options less than 30 days in duration, alleging that the longer-term contracts were more advantageous to the public. More recently options of three months or less have been replaced by longer-term contracts. Options contracts of six months and ten days are now the most popular maturity, since this maturity allows the holder to take advantage of the capital gains provisions of the income tax laws. (The tax treatment of stock options will be explained in Section 2.5.)

It appears that interest in stock options is an increasing function of bullish activity in the stock market, as evidenced by increased activity and rising stock prices. During the 1937–1942 bear market, yearly option volume declined from 2.2 million shares to 0.7 million shares. The strong bull market of the 1950's, however, was accompanied by a substantial increase in option volume. In Figure 1-1 option sales and stock price movements from 1942 through 1960 are charted.

Despite the large increase in option volume, the number of

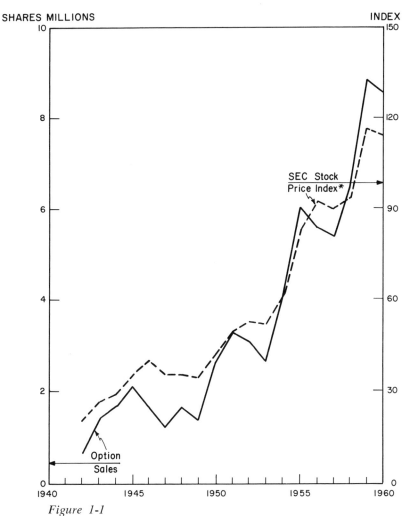

Figure 1-1

Volume of options sold compared with stock price movements, 1942–1960.

SOURCE: Securities and Exchange Commission, *Report on Put and Call Options,* p. 21.

dealers during recent years has been much lower than during the early years of the PCBDA. In 1940 there were 40 members of the Association, but the membership declined to 28 in 1961. The Securities and Exchange Commission reported that only 15 of the 28 firms were actively engaged in trading of options.[23] There are two general types of option houses. The first group of firms perform purely a brokerage service; they act as middlemen between the option sellers (writers) and option buyers. The second group of firms act in the capacity of dealers as well. These firms are willing to take positions in options for their own account and risk, whereas the former type acquire and sell all options on the same day. The five firms that acted both as brokers and dealers accounted for 75 per cent of all option sales during the month of June 1959.

Generally, writers of options are individual investors with large portfolios who own the securities upon which the options are written. The volume of options written by Stock Exchange firms and Put and Call dealers has been very small.[24] There has been little institutional involvement in the option writing. For example, tax-exempt institutions have not generally been involved in option writing, in part because of special tax problems to be discussed later. Most buyers of options are also individuals but, unlike the option writers, buyers tend to be small investors rather than professionals.[25] It appears that the major motivation of option buyers is the desire to speculate with a small amount of capital. Only a limited volume of options has actually been used for hedging purposes (e.g., to protect a long position in a security the owner may buy a Put option). Institutions generally do not buy options and there has been little trading in options by corporate insiders, although in recent years there have been some notable and well publicized exceptions.

One recent development in the market deserves special mention. As of the end of 1968, one New York Stock Exchange member firm, Goodbody and Co., has begun to make continuous markets on options in a limited number of actually traded issues. Goodbody stands ready to purchase options from prospective writers at its bid price

---

[23] SEC, *Put and Call Options,* p. 63.
[24] *Ibid.,* pp. 55–56.
[25] *Ibid.,* pp. 74–77.

and to offer options to prospective buyers at its offer price. This represents the first attempt to establish an organized, continuous dealer market in options.

Apart from the individual option writers and buyers and the firms acting as dealers or brokers, there are two important additional participants in the option market: the endorsers and the converters. All option contracts are endorsed by member firms of the New York Stock Exchange. The endorsement guarantees the performance of the contract and makes the option a negotiable instrument. The endorsing broker usually receives a fee of $6.25 or $12.50 per option for his services. In addition, the dealer or broker himself collects a commission for the service of bringing the option writer and buyer together. Because of these commissions and fees, the price paid by the option buyer is generally more than that received by the option writer. For a typical $50 stock, option firms estimate that this spread has averaged $62.50 per 100 shares ($\frac{5}{8}$ of one point) during recent years.

To understand the function of the option converter one must first observe that, at least during recent periods, option traders have been characteristically bullish concerning the prospects for the stock market. Thus, option buyers have preferred, other considerations being equal, to purchase Call rather than Put options. On the other hand, option sellers have preferred to issue Straddles rather than Call options, especially since, as will be explained in the next chapter, the Straddle writer need put up neither more securities nor more margin than the Call writer, whereas the premium received is substantially larger.[26] In fact, most Put options arise from the writing of Straddles. Thus if Put and Call premiums were equal, there would tend to be an excess supply of Puts. As a result, the price of Call options is greater than the price of Puts, and the practice of "option conversion" has developed.

An option converter literally converts Put options into Calls. He accomplishes this by simultaneously buying a Put, buying 100 shares of the stock, and selling a Call on the same stock with the same

---

[26] See Section 2.2. Moreover, the writer who owns the stock in question can sell a Straddle as easily as he can sell a Call. He must simply deposit his shares as security for the transaction.

maturity as the Put. The contract price of the Put and Call must be the same as the market price of the stock purchased. By these transactions the converter is perfectly hedged against stock price changes in either direction. As long as he holds the stock and the Put until the expiration date of the Call option, the converter cannot lose. For example, suppose the converter buys 100 shares of stock at $50 per share, purchases a Put option at $450, and sells a Call option at $587.50. If the stock goes down the Call will remain unexercised, and the converter can exercise his Put. His profit, net of commissions and carrying costs, is equal to the difference between the Put and Call premiums. The same result follows for increases in stock prices as well. Consequently, the possibility of option arbitrage sets a ceiling to the spread between Put and Call premiums. For their service, converters charge a rate of interest at least $\frac{1}{2}$ of 1 per cent above the broker's loan rate (on the funds needed to purchase the stock) plus expenses.

Further light may be shed on the organization of the market by the study, already referred to, conducted by the SEC of all options outstanding on June 1, 1959.[27] Outstanding Call options covered nearly twice as many shares on that date as did Put options. Approximately 70 per cent of the Puts were held by firms who had converted them into Call options. About 80 per cent of the outstanding options had been originally written with an expiration date of six months or longer. More than three quarters of all the options outstanding were for one hundred shares. Only 21 options covered as many as one thousand shares. In most stock price ranges about one third of the stocks on the New York Exchange were under option. The only important exceptions were shares selling for under $10, which were too low-priced for the option market's minimum premium of $137.50 (and consequently only 15 per cent of the shares in this group were under option) and shares selling in the $80–$100 range. Included in the latter group were most of the "high flyers" of the time, and about 50 per cent of these issues were under option. Option activity was highly concentrated, however, in the most actively traded stocks. Of the 1087 common stocks listed on the New York Stock Exchange

---

[27] SEC, *Report on Put and Call Options*, pp. 26 ff.

during June 1959, the 187 most active securities accounted for 75.4 per cent of all option activity.

1.4
The Profitability of Dealing in Options

Apart from purely descriptive treatments, previous studies of the option market may be subsumed under two categories.[28] First, there have been a number of studies, essentially statistical in character, which have sought to determine whether an investor who engaged in repeated option transactions over a period of years would have found some particular form of contract to be profitable. Second, there have been studies which utilize standard capital theory and the random-walk theory of stock prices[29] to build a theoretical model of stock-option value. In this section some results of the first group of studies are presented.

In order to assess the rationality of option dealing by undertaking a statistical analysis of the option market, several studies have compared the average payoffs from option buying with the actual cost of such options. The results of these studies have been contradictory. Kruizenga, studying the period 1946–1956, found that the buying of 6-month Calls would have yielded an average annual profit of 35 per cent.[30] Boness, looking at actual transactions during the 1957–1960 period, found that continuous option buying in either Puts or Calls would have resulted in large net losses, but that option writers, by utilizing certain strategies, could have realized gains that moderately exceeded the gains from diversified equity investments over the same period.[31] Katz, in a study of a sample of option contracts written over a 21-month period, April 22, 1960 to January

---

[28] Much of the recent scientific work in this area has been collected in Paul H. Cootner ed., *The Random Character of Stock Market Prices* (Cambridge: M.I.T. Press, 1964), Part IV.

[29] A study of stock options provided the original motivation for a statistical study of speculative prices. See Louis Bachelier, "Theory of Speculation," *ibid.,* pp. 17–75.

[30] Richard J. Kruizenga, "Profit Returns from Purchasing Puts and Calls," *ibid.,* pp. 392–411.

[31] A. James Boness, "Some Evidence on the Profitability of Trading in Put and Call Options," *ibid.,* pp. 475–496. Explanations of the various option contracts from the standpoint of both buyer and writer will be offered in the next chapter.

30, 1962, found that option writing was mildly unprofitable.[32] As a group the option writers considered in the study had an average loss of 0.1 per cent. Taking the Boness and Katz results alone, one would be tempted to conclude that the only participants in the option market who have found option dealing profitable have been the option brokers and dealers who collect a spread between the price received by the option seller and that received by the option buyer.

These empirical studies do not inspire much confidence in their results, however, nor do they clarify the question of the rationality of option dealing. Apart from the obvious difficulty that these studies use data from different time periods and thus cannot be compared directly, several other problems affect their analysis. The data on option premiums used in these studies have typically been based on nominal rather than real quotations. Data from the quotation sheets of option dealers and from their newspaper advertisements represent only bids and offers, which may be far from the prices of actual trades. Moreover, some studies have calculated the profits from option dealing assuming away the existence of transactions charges,[33] and all have ignored taxes. We shall show in the next chapter that brokerage and other transactions fees and personal income taxes significantly affect the relative payoffs from alternative option strategies. Finally, on a more fundamental level, these studies do not really analyze the ultimate rationality of option dealing.

It is not legitimate to assess investor rationality by observing a time series of average outcomes. Consider, for example, the case of an investor who owns a security and purchases a Put option on it in order to obtain insurance, that is, to hedge against a decline in the market value of the stock over the option period. The failure to exercise this option prior to its expiration date (as would occur if the market price of the stock went up) cannot be taken as an example of an unsuccessful investment strategy any more than the failure to collect damages under a fire insurance policy can be considered as indicating an irrational strategy for the home-owner if his house fails to burn down. Moreover, for an individual who buys a Call option

---

[32] Richard Katz, "The Profitability of Put and Call Option Writing," *Industrial Management Review* (Fall 1963), pp. 55–69.

[33] See, for example, Kruizenga, in Cootner ed., *Stock Market Prices*.

purely for speculation, the act may be perfectly rational even if the expected value of the option is less than the purchase price. It is entirely plausible that the investor's utility function is such that even a very small chance of the large gain more than compensates in utility value for a large chance of a small loss.

1.5
Previous Theoretical Studies

Most studies concerned with the theoretical valuation of securities are based on calculation of the expected value of the security in question. The security may differ from case to case and, indeed, there are studies dealing with the value of such securities as common stocks, convertible bonds, Put and Call options, and warrants.[34] In the simplest terms, what these studies have in common is that, for each possible level of common stock prices, P, they derive the value of the security in question, $V(P)$, posit the existence of a probability distribution over stock prices, $F(P)$, and finally compute the expected value of the security by

$$E(V) = \int V(P)\,dF(P) \qquad (1.1)$$

The various studies differ in their specification of the theoretical model, which leads to a determination of $V(P)$, and of the stochastic part of the model, which affects $F(P)$. A few illustrations may convey the flavor of these arguments.

A convertible debenture is a bond which, at the option of the holder, may be converted into a stated number of shares of common stock. Let

C be the value of the convertible.

B be the bond value of the convertible (that is, the value of an

---

[34] A. W. Harbaugh, "Expected Value of Options, Warrants and Convertible Securities," paper presented at the 27th National Meeting of the Operations Research Society of America, Boston, May 1965, pp. 1–38; W. J. Baumol, B. G. Malkiel, and R. E. Quandt, "The Valuation of Convertible Securities," *Quarterly J. of Economics* (February 1966) pp. 48–59; A. James Boness, "Elements of a Theory of Stock-Option Value," *J. of Political Economy* (April 1964) pp. 163–175; Case M. Sprenkle, "Warrant Prices as Indicators of Expectations and Preferences," *Yale Economic Essays,* Vol. 1, No. 2 (1961) pp. 178–231; Paul A. Samuelson, "Rational Theory of Warrant Pricing," *Industrial Management Review* (Spring 1965) pp. 13–32.

equivalent security divested of its convertibility feature), assumed constant for the sake of simplicity.

P_t be the price of the underlying common stock at time t.

S_t be the common-stock equivalent value of the convertible; that is, S_t/P_t = constant = the number of shares into which a debenture may be converted.

P_t^r be the price at time t relative to some base period price P_0, i.e., $P_t^r = P_t/P_0$.

According to Baumol, Malkiel, and Quandt the value of the convertible at time $t = 0$ is at least as great as: (1) the value of the stock equivalent S_0 at that time plus the expected value of the protection provided by the convertible against declines of the stock price; and (2) the bond value of the convertible plus the expected value of a call on the common stock. Thus,

$$C = \max (C_b, C_s) \qquad (1.2)$$

where

$$C_b = S_0 + \int_0^{B/S_0} (B - S_t) \, dF(P_t^r)$$

$$C_s = B + \int_{B/S_0}^{\infty} (S_t - B) \, dF(P_t^r)$$

and $F(P_t^r)$ is the probability distribution of the future stock price relative to the base period price.

A somewhat similar expected-value approach to Put and Call options is taken by Harbaugh and Boness. If the price of the stock is below the striking price, the value of the Call to the purchaser is zero. If the market price P_t is above the striking price P_0, the individual's gain from a Call on 100 shares is $100(P_t - P_0)$, where we disregard commissions and other transactions costs for the sake of simplicity. Denoting the value of the Call at a price of P_t by

$$V(P_t) = 100(P_t - P_0) \quad \text{if } P_t > P_0$$

$$V(P_t) = 0 \qquad\qquad\quad \text{otherwise,}$$

the expected value of exercising the Call then is

$$E(V) = \int V(P_t) \, dF(P_t^r) \qquad (1.3)$$

where, as before, $F(P_t^r)$ is the distribution of P_t/P_0 and may also be regarded as the conditional distribution of P_t given P_0. The expected

22

value of the Call may then be computed as the difference between the expected value of exercising the Call and the cost of the option contract.

Boness's approach is basically similar. The expected value of a Call is the difference between the expected value of exercising the option and its cost. The former, in turn, is

$$E(V|P_t > P_0) \cdot p + E(V|P_t \leq P_0)(1 - p) \tag{1.4}$$

where p is the probability that $P_t > P_0$. Since $E(V|P_t \leq P_0) = 0$, the Harbaugh and Boness models reduce to identical formulations. Furthermore, both of them assume that utility is linear in money; Harbaugh does so implicitly and Boness explicitly by assuming that traders are indifferent to risk. In addition, Boness assumes that stock prices are expected to increase at a constant exponential rate: $P_t = P_0 e^{rt}$. The unknown rate of appreciation of stock prices is estimated to be the rate that makes the actual market prices of Call options consistent with their theoretical values. Boness finds that option buyers apparently have expected a rate of appreciation from common stocks of 22 per cent per annum compounded continuously.

Other writers have formulated similar kinds of models but have utilized their theoretical and empirical work primarily as a means of measuring investor attitudes toward risk. Rosett,[35] for example, uses a model like that of Boness but extrapolates the expected rate of appreciation and other moments of the distribution of expected future stock prices. On the basis of these moments, Rosett finds that the actuarial values of stock options tend to be less than their market prices. Assuming that investors behave rationally, the reasons for the purchase of options must lie in the characteristics of the buyers' utility functions. Rosett conjectures that option buyers may have cubic utility functions. They prefer high expected values, dislike variance, and like positive skewness.[36] Rosett suggests that even

---

[35] Richard Rosett, "Estimating the Utility of Wealth from Call Option Transactions." In Donald Hester and James Tobin, *Risk Aversion and Portfolio Choice* (New York: Wiley, 1967) pp. 154–169.

[36] These conjectures are supported by Alvin K. Klevorick, "Capital Budgeting Under Risk: A Mathematical-Programming Approach," Econometric Research Program, Research Memorandum No. 89, Princeton University, September 1967. An elegant axiomatic approach allows Klevorick to deduce a cubic utility function which has the characteristic that utility increases with positive skewness.

higher moments may be important in explaining investor behavior in the option market.[37]

These theoretical and more sophisticated empirical studies suffer from many of the same defects as the more descriptive empirical studies we reviewed in the preceding section. Specifically, transactions costs and taxes are ignored, and the prices used to represent market values are often nominal rather than real. In addition, all previous theoretical work seems to have treated specific securities or investment alternatives in isolation from others and has made almost no attempt to integrate option dealing with the menu of choices available to the investor in the general securities market. We feel that this particular shortcoming of previous theoretical models is a serious one, as can be seen from the following argument: The potential option buyer has several alternatives available for speculation on the short-term prospects for an individual security. He may buy stock directly, buy the stock on margin, buy a Call option, write a Put option, buy convertible bonds if they are available, or employ some combination of these strategies. If we postulate a specific set of expectations (and a particular utility surface) on the part of the decision maker, will Call options necessarily be chosen over alternative investment strategies? For example, if an investor really does expect the price of a stock to increase at a rate of 22 per cent per annum, why would a Call option be chosen over the strategy of buying stock on margin, that is, borrowing some of the funds needed to pay for the shares, thus increasing the investor's leverage? For some margin requirements, it can be shown that buying stock on margin would provide an investor an expected return on his investment greater than that for a Call while subjecting him to less risk (variance of return). Therefore, we believe that the question of the ultimate rationality of option dealing or dealing in any one security can not be answered by the types of models we have been describing.

---

[37] Other studies have employed stock warrants (a type of long-term Call option where the contract price is typically small compared with the market price of the common shares) to help identify investor attitudes toward risk. Sprenkle, "Warrant Prices," finds no evidence of either risk aversion or risk-loving on the part of warrant buyers. Ayres, on the other hand, finds that the risk premiums demanded by warrant purchasers appear to be very large. See Herbert F. Ayres, "Risk Aversions in the Warrant Markets," *Industrial Management Review* (Fall 1963) pp. 45–53.

The predictions of these theoretical models will, of course, also depend upon the assumptions made about $F(P_t^r)$, the distribution of relative stock prices. The question of what to use for $F(P_t^r)$ can be approached in several ways. Baumol, Malkiel, and Quandt do not commit themselves as to the theoretical form of $F(P_t^r)$ and are content to compute the value of a convertible security by employing a discrete approximation to their valuation formula in which $F(P_t^r)$ is replaced by an empirically observed frequency distribution. Harbaugh, Boness, Rosett and others all assume in one form or another that relative stock prices, P_t/P_0, are lognormally distributed, which is a consequence of the more fundamental assumption that stock prices perform a proportionate random walk (that is, a random walk in the logarithm of prices).

Since the distributions employed in these analyses are distributions of stock prices *relative* to the price in some base period, one has to make some assumption concerning the investor's horizon or, equivalently, the choice of the base period. Baumol, Malkiel, and Quandt employ, alternately, a two- and three-year horizon. The Harbaugh and Boness models are consistent with any finite horizon in view of the assumption that the variance of the distribution is proportional to the length of the horizon. This assumption, together with the assumption that the logarithms of price relatives are normally distributed with zero mean, has the consequence that the mean of the price relatives themselves is an increasing function of the horizon. The implied trend in stock price changes will induce the holder of a Call option not to exercise it before the expiration date of the contract, if at all. This supports a choice of a horizon equal to the expiration date of the option contract.

An alternative approach to choosing the distribution of stock price changes and one of considerable theoretical significance rests on the observation that many economic quantities, and specifically certain speculative prices, seem to behave as if they were generated by distributions with infinite variances. This conjecture has led Mandelbrot and others to present elegant treatments of the stable Paretian distributions, which are the only distributions of this type to have all of several highly desirable statistical properties, such as being the limiting distributions of sums of independently distributed random variables.[38]

The hypothesis that speculative prices are drawings from a stable Paretian distribution with an infinite second moment has been argued forcefully but nevertheless the issue remains open.[39] As a matter of fact, the evidence from the failure of sample second moments to settle down to some limiting value as they are computed from longer and longer realizations of a time series is consistent with the notion of a nonstationary stochastic process and does not imply that the corresponding ensemble moments would behave in the same manner. On the basis of the evidence to date, we feel that the stable Paretian hypothesis is neither proved nor a theoretically essential ingredient of a model of security values.

What is perhaps even more important in our framework than the precise nature of the distribution that generates stock prices is the set of attitudes (or lack thereof) that investors exhibit toward future stock values. The rationality of their decisions must be judged not in terms of what distribution in fact prevails but in terms of the price-distributional information that can possibly be available to them. Since our basic position is that the average investor will characteristically have little or no information available as to the probability of various short-term price fluctuations, the specific distributional assumptions of the various random-walk theories are largely irrelevant for our purposes.

1.6
A Cross-Sectional Analysis
of Option Premiums

In this section we present the results of a cross-sectional study of the ratios of the option premium to the price of the underlying common stock for a sample of Call options and Straddles. The purpose of this study is twofold: first, our results on how options are

---

[38] Benoit Mandelbrot, "The Variation of Certain Speculative Markets," *J. of Business* (Oct. 1963) pp. 394–419; Eugene F. Fama, "Mandelbrot and the Stable Paretian Hypothesis," *J. of Business* (Oct. 1963) pp. 420–429.

[39] For a somewhat skeptical attitude concerning these arguments see Paul H. Cootner, "Comments on the Variation of Certain Speculative Prices," in *Stock Market Prices,* pp. 333–337.

priced are important for completing our general description of the market and of the determination of option premiums, and second, we shall need to employ the estimates presented below in our study of optimal investor strategies in the option market.

The preceding discussion has suggested a number of variables that might be expected to influence the ratio of a Call premium to the price of the underlying common stock. The most important are the following.

1. The expected rate of appreciation of the common stock. We would expect Calls to be more attractive to option buyers for stocks that promised a relatively large rate of price appreciation. The expected value of the proceeds from exercising a Call will increase directly with the rate of stock-price appreciation. This is particularly clear in the Boness formulation described in the preceding Section.

2. The variance of stock prices. Other things being equal, we would also expect the value of a Call-option premium to increase with an increase in the expected variance of the underlying stock. This can easily be illustrated with the work of Baumol, Malkiel, and Quandt on the worth of the convertibility option for convertible debentures. The greater the expected variance of stock prices, the mean of the distribution remaining the same, the greater will be both the expected value of the call on the common stock and the worth of the protection offered by the debenture's bond value should the common stock decline. This argument carries over to regular Call options, since no matter how much the underlying common stock declines the option buyer can lose no more than the Call premium.

3. Trading volume. A number of market practitioners have suggested that the trading volume of the underlying common stock may influence the value of the option premium. They suggested that Call buyers prefer to buy options on securities that have only a small number of shares outstanding. The argument is that the smaller the number of shares outstanding, the more likely it is that a piece of good news will have a large effect on the market price. It is also argued that option buyers prefer a situation where the ratio of shares traded to shares outstanding is relatively large. The preference for dealing in securities that have a relatively large turnover is explained

by the belief that rather inactively traded securities may not respond to general market movements. Recapitulating the argument, it is said that the (percentage) option premium should be negatively related to the number of shares outstanding and positively related to the turnover ratio.

4. The absolute market price of the underlying shares. Market practitioners have also suggested that the absolute price of the under-lying shares will influence the option premium. Specifically, they feel that the ratio of the option premium to the market price of the shares should vary inversely with the absolute price of the shares. The ex-planation is that option buyers are assumed to prefer to put at risk only a small sum of money. Suppose that the premiums on all six-month Call options amounted to 10 per cent of the price of the shares. For a stock selling at $20 a share an option on 100 shares would cost only $200. For a stock selling at $500 per share, however, a 100-share option would cost $5000, which is a substantial invest-ment. Consequently, those individuals whose motive in buying options is to speculate on a small amount of capital will prefer, other con-siderations being equal, to buy options on the $20 stock rather than on the shares selling at $500, if both option premiums amount to the same fraction of the stock price.

These general beliefs about the pricing of Call options can easily be formulated as testable hypotheses. Employing the defini-tions contained in Table 1-3 and assuming that the relationship be-tween the ratio of the Call premium to the market price (C/P) and the explanatory variable is approximately linear, we may write

$$\frac{C}{P} = a_0 + \overset{+}{a_1}V + \overset{-}{a_2}T_1 + \overset{+}{a_3}T_2 + \overset{+}{a_4}g + \overset{-}{a_5}P \tag{1.5}$$

The signs above each coefficient indicate the average way in which we would expect the independent variables to influence Call-option premiums. We would expect that C/P would be positively related to the past volatility of stock prices, the turnover ratio, and the expected rate of price appreciation of the underlying common stock; and negatively related to the number of shares outstanding and the abso-lute price of the shares.

28

Table 1-3

Variables Employed in Cross-Sectional Study of Option Premiums

Variable	Source and/or Method of Calculation
C = Call premium paid to writer	Option brokers and dealers
S = Straddle premium paid to writer	Option brokers and dealers
V = Past volatility of stock prices	$\sum\limits_{t=T-10}^{T-1} \left(\dfrac{P_H - P_L}{1/2(P_H + P_L)} \right)_t,$ where P_H and P_L are the yearly high and low stock prices from Standard & Poor's Compustat tape and T is 1964 or 1965 or 1966.
T_1 = Number of shares outstanding at end of year (in hundreds of millions)	Compustat tape
T_2 = Turnover ratio (ratio of shares traded to shares outstanding)	Compustat tape
P = Price of shares on date option was written	Option brokers and dealers
g = Expected long-term growth rate for earnings of underlying common shares (proxy for expected rate of price appreciation)	Expectations of a sample of security analysts
Y = Dummy variable for year of observation	Year option written minus 1960. N.B. Options written from Nov. 1, 1964 through Jan. 30, 1965 are considered year-end 1964 options.

Equations were also estimated for the premium-to-price ratios of Straddles. The test equation employed was the same as that for Calls except that g, the expected rate of appreciation of the stock price, was omitted. While a higher expected rate of price appreciation would tend to enhance the value of the Call part of the Straddle, it could be expected to have a negative effect on the Put part. Equation 1.6 shows the relationship used to explain S/P together with the expected signs of the coefficients.

$$\frac{S}{P} = b_0 + \overset{+}{b_1}V + \overset{-}{b_2}T_1 + \overset{+}{b_3}T_2 + \overset{-}{b_4}P \tag{1.6}$$

29

The data employed in the tests consisted of a sample of prices paid to writers of 106 Call options and 61 Straddles during the year-end periods of 1964, 1965, and 1966. The year-end period, November 1 through January 31, was chosen for the study because certain data concerning expectations were employed together with the option premiums, and these expectational data were available only annually as of mid-December for the three years. The expectations employed were forecasts of the future growth rates of earnings per share made by a sample of security analysts.[40] These forecasts were used as the nearest proxy available for the expected rate of price appreciation. Sources and the methods of calculation for the other variables employed in the study are described in Table 1-3.

The results of the cross-sectional study are contained in Tables 1-4 and 1-5. Equations were first estimated for each year separately,

Table 1-4

Regression Results: Premiums on Call Options, 1964–1966 Year-End Periods

$$\frac{C}{P} = a_0 + a_1 V + a_2 T_1 + a_3 T_2 + a_4 g + a_5 P + a_6 Y$$

Year	$\hat{a}_0$	$\hat{a}_1$	$\hat{a}_2$	$\hat{a}_3$	$\hat{a}_4$	$\hat{a}_5$	$\hat{a}_6$	r^2
1964	.088	.011	−.006	.005	.058	−.016		.720
		(.007)	(.002)	(.005)	(.046)	(.006)		
1965	.085	.018	−.004	.022	.055	−.015		.794
		(.003)	(.002)	(.008)	(.040)	(.005)		
1966	.082	.027	−.004	.010	.202	−.023		.635
		(.015)	(.002)	(.004)	(.065)	(.013)		
1964–1966	.058	.019	−.005	.010	.069	−.015	.006	.719
		(.002)	(.001)	(.002)	(.027)	(.004)	(.001)	

and then the data for all three years were combined in one equation. For the aggregate equation a dummy variable was added to estimate the effect on the constant term of the year in which the data were

---

[40] The option prices were furnished by option brokers who wished to remain anonymous. For a description of the expectational data and of how they were collected, see John G. Cragg and Burton G. Malkiel, "The Consensus and Accuracy of Some Predictions of the Growth of Corporate Earnings," *J. of Finance* (March 1968) pp. 67–84.

collected. We note from the tables that the signs of all the coefficients are as expected and that in most cases the coefficients are significantly

Table 1-5

Regression Results: Premiums on Straddle Options, 1964–1966 Year-End Periods

$$\frac{S}{P} = b_0 + b_1 V + b_2 T_1 + b_3 T_2 + b_4 P + b_5 Y$$

Year	$\hat{b}_0$	$\hat{b}_1$	$\hat{b}_2$	$\hat{b}_3$	$\hat{b}_4$	$\hat{b}_5$	r^2
1964	.135	.036	−.011	.005	−.020		.781
		(.013)	(.003)	(.007)	(.009)		
1965	.126	.054	−.008	.018	−.026		.858
		(.007)	(.019)	(.017)	(.012)		
1966	.122	.059	−.006	.024	−.020		.795
		(.038)	(.003)	(.009)	(.021)		
1964–1966	.106	.049	−.008	.017	−.019	.004	.808
		(.005)	(.002)	(.004)	(.006)	(.002)	

different from zero. In the regressions in which three years' data are pooled, the T statistic is highest for the volatility variable for both Calls and Straddles.[41]

1.7
The Focus of the Present Study

It is clear from this discussion of the option market and the review of the literature that many questions are left unanswered. Specifically, neither the empirical academic studies nor the nostrums for market success offered by practitioners offer much help to the potential investor in formulating an optimal investment strategy. He is told alternatively that option buying is profitable, option writing is profitable, or that both are unprofitable. Some studies have suggested

---

[41] We tried to include measures of the variance and skewness of past returns on the common stock in place of the volatility measure reported in the tables. We found, however, that the coefficient of the skewness variable was never significant in the regression for Calls. In the regression for Straddles the skewness was occasionally significant but the sign of its coefficient varied from year to year. These two variables together contributed less to an explanation of the option premiums than the crude volatility measure we employed. It may well be that the crude measure may better represent the expectations of option buyers.

that activities in the option markets should be undertaken only by investors with particular utility surfaces. In this connection, some practitioners in the market have argued that the best use of option contracts is to provide "insurance" protection. The difficulty is that an investor is provided no guidance in formulating an optimal investment strategy.

In addition, previous work has made almost no attempt to integrate option dealing with the choices open to the investor in the general securities market. Moreover, crucially important phenomena such as taxes and the brokerage charges involved in consummating option transactions are often completely ignored. When options are placed within the more general framework of the securities market as a whole, and when taxes and actual costs of undertaking various transactions are included, there arise questions such as the following: (1) Is dealing in Put and Call options ever an optimal strategy for an individual investor? (2) Can a given individual's market position be explained only by making specific assumptions about his utility function and his expectations as to future price changes? The general approach of this study will be to perform computer experiments which simulate a variety of market conditions and different states of expectations, employ various criteria of investor rationality under uncertainty, and hypothesize various kinds of utility functions on the part of investors. We shall then determine which investment strategy is optimal under the conditions postulated. In this way we shall try to ascertain the proper role of stock options in an investor's portfolio.

The type of experiment we wish to perform may be described briefly as follows. Suppose some representative security sells at $50 and that the range of possible future (six months later) prices at which the security may sell is expected to be between $40 and $60. Further assume that a number of pure investment strategies are available to an investor, such as buying stock, buying Call options, writing Put options, buying six-month Treasury bills, and so forth. Postulate a variety of hypothetical alternative utility functions for the investor involving, for example, linearity in money gains, or mildly (sharply) diminishing marginal utility of money payoffs. Assume finally that the investor is completely ignorant about the relative probability of the occurrence of alternative possible prices.[42] The situation may then be correctly described as a game against nature. We feel that this way of looking at the investment problem is an important contribution of this study, an aspect which differentiates it sharply from other approaches. The questions we seek to answer include: What will be the optimal strategy for an investor utilizing alternative decision rules for solving the game against nature? Will mixed strategies be optimal? What difference will it make if the investor does hold a subjective (prior) probability distribution over alternative states of nature, perhaps one based on past distributions of stock price changes? The answers to several of the questions raised above may not only clear up many of the puzzling questions raised in the current literature, but should also serve to integrate the theory of option trading within the general framework of the securities market.

---

[42] An objection may be raised that in reality investors are rarely completely ignorant. Our position is not that one may not assume that investors possess some prior distribution over the states of nature but rather that interesting cases also occur if we posit complete ignorance.

CHAPTER TWO

Alternative Strategies
Available to the Investor

We have indicated that almost all previous studies of stock options have treated options in isolation. No attempts seem to have been made to consider the rationality of option dealing in a general context of stock market trading. In reality, an individual can undertake a number of different actions. If he is confident about the prospects for a particular company, he can purchase common shares in the company directly. On the other hand, if he wants a more levered position he may buy shares on margin, borrowing some funds from his broker to pay for the shares. Indeed, an investor might employ any one of several alternative market strategies to take a speculative position in a particular stock. Thus it seems imperative to consider option trading as only one of a number of different market strategies. If option trading is rational at all, it must be rational in the sense that option strategies are optimal by some criteria when considered against the other alternatives open to the investor.

2.1
Introduction

We assume that the representative investor may utilize any one or any combination of sixteen particular investment strategies. This chapter is devoted to a description of these strategies. The strategies are listed in Table 2-1 with a brief description of the investor's position under each. The table uses a vector notation, which will be discussed at greater length in 2.3.8, indicating how the investor is

Table 2-1

The Sixteen Strategies

Strategy			Description of Investor's Position	
1	C	Cash	Zero position	$\begin{bmatrix} 0 \\ 0 \end{bmatrix}$
2	BS	Buy Stock	Long. Own stock	$\begin{bmatrix} +1 \\ -1 \end{bmatrix}$
3	SS	Sell Stock (Short)	Short. Owe stock	$\begin{bmatrix} -1 \\ +1 \end{bmatrix}$
4	BSM	Buy Stock on Margin	Long. Own stock on margin	$\begin{bmatrix} +1 \\ -1 \end{bmatrix}$
5	SSM	Sell Stock (Short) on Margin	Short. Owe stock on margin	$\begin{bmatrix} -1 \\ +1 \end{bmatrix}$
6	BC	Buy Call	Long. Own right to buy stock at a fixed price	$\begin{bmatrix} +1 \\ 0 \end{bmatrix}$
7	BP	Buy Put	Short. Own right to sell stock at a fixed price	$\begin{bmatrix} 0 \\ +1 \end{bmatrix}$
8	BSTR	Buy Straddle	Long. Own right to buy stock at a fixed price; Short. Own right to sell stock at a fixed price	$\begin{bmatrix} +1 \\ +1 \end{bmatrix}$
9	SC,BS	Sell (Write) Call Buy Stock	Long. Own stock; Short. Obligation to sell stock at a fixed price	$\begin{bmatrix} 0 \\ -1 \end{bmatrix}$
10	SP,BS	Sell (Write) Put Buy Stock	Long. Own stock; Long. Obligation to buy stock at a fixed price	$\begin{bmatrix} +1 \\ -2 \end{bmatrix}$
11	SC	Sell Call	Short. Obligation to sell stock at a fixed price	$\begin{bmatrix} -1 \\ 0 \end{bmatrix}$
12	SP	Sell Put	Long. Obligation to buy stock at a fixed price	$\begin{bmatrix} 0 \\ -1 \end{bmatrix}$
13	SSTR,BS	Sell Straddle (Call and Put) Buy Stock	Long. Own stock; Long. Obligation to buy stock at a fixed price; Short. Obligation to sell stock at a fixed price	$\begin{bmatrix} 0 \\ -2 \end{bmatrix}$
14	SSTR	Sell Straddle	Long. Obligation to buy stock at a fixed price; Short. Obligation to sell stock at a fixed price	$\begin{bmatrix} -1 \\ -1 \end{bmatrix}$
15	BS,BP	Buy Stock Buy Put	Long. Own stock; Short. Own right to sell stock at a fixed price	$\begin{bmatrix} +1 \\ 0 \end{bmatrix}$
16	SS,BC	Sell Stock Buy Call	Short. Owe stock; Long. Own right to buy stock at a fixed price	$\begin{bmatrix} 0 \\ +1 \end{bmatrix}$

affected by stock price changes. Briefly, the upper element in the vector indicates how an investor is affected by an upward movement in stock price. If that element is unity, he benefits; if it is -1, he loses; if it is 0, he is unaffected. The lower element shows how he is affected by downward price movements, using the same notation.

The number of strategies, sixteen, was chosen as the result of a compromise between two conflicting goals. We wanted to consider all major alternative investment strategies; yet in the interest of economy we tried to subsume similar strategies under one category. For example, Strategy 1, Cash, as defined here will be seen actually to be composed of a combination of several alternative investment strategies utilizing different types of debt instruments. Moreover, we have had to ignore completely several investment strategies such as those involving the use of convertible bonds, warrants, and other investment instruments. The sixteen strategies treated, however, are sufficiently broad to cover the major alternatives considered by most investors.

2.2
Assumptions Used To Calculate Payoffs
from the Investment Strategies

In order to calculate the potential returns available to an investor who employs each of the sixteen investment strategies, the following specific assumptions will be made initially:

1. A typical $50 stock will be used as the object of investment in all our examples. In deriving returns, the security will be assumed to fluctuate within a range of at most 30 points above and below the initial price of $50.

2. In any strategy involving the buying or selling of stock, actual transactions costs — commissions, transfer taxes, and SEC fees — will be used in making specific payoff calculations.[1] In cases where the investor borrows money from his broker, typical margin requirements and interest rates in existence during the early 1960's will be employed.

---

[1] These brokerage charges, transfer taxes, etc., are those that prevailed on the New York Stock Exchange during the 1960–1964 period.

3. The investor has enough cash to deal in round lots (lots of 100 shares). While all payoffs will be calculated per dollar of investment, the per dollar brokerage costs are slightly larger if the investor purchases less than a 100-share lot.

4. When Put and Call strategies are employed, typical premiums for six-month ten-day (190-day) options will be used in making the calculations. These prices have been obtained from the records of several option firms. They are intended to represent the average premiums paid during the 1960 through 1964 period for a typical $50 stock.

5. All transactions assume a 190-day holding period. The investor is assumed to take no action within the holding period.

6. The stock in question pays no dividends during the holding period.

7. The investor begins the investment period with a portfolio consisting entirely of cash and closes out any long or short position at the end of the 190-day holding period, so that his final position consists entirely of cash. We call this the "cash-to-cash" case.

8. The investor pays no taxes on his gains and receives no tax rebate on his losses. We call this the tax-exempt case.

Several of these assumptions are altered in later experiments. Specifically, later in this chapter we shall examine the effect of taxes and dividends on the investor's returns. Moreover, in some experiments we allow the investor to begin and end the 190-day holding period with a portfolio of stock rather than cash. The present section abstracts from these complications in order to show the fundamentals of option strategies more clearly.

Assumption 5 is maintained throughout most of the analysis and requires further comment. This assumption allows the representative investor no freedom of action within the 190-day holding period. If the investor buys a 190-day Call option, he can only exercise the option on the expiration date. Thus if the common stock goes up 20 points during the option period, he is not allowed to close out his position at a profit. Rather, with the exceptions that will be described later, he must await the end of the holding period before taking any action whatsoever.

It might seem that this simplifying assumption makes our model diverge widely from reality. In fact, the available evidence suggests that this assumption may conform closely to actual practice. In their study of the securities option market, for example, the Securities and Exchange Commission found that approximately 75 per cent of all Call options that were exercised were exercised on their expiration date or less than a week before expiration.[2] This is especially true for over-six-months options, as will be indicated later (see Section 2.5). The investor who waits until at least six months have passed before exercising his option will obtain a substantial tax benefit.[3] Moreover, as was mentioned in Section 1.5, an assumption that stock price relatives are lognormally distributed with zero mean implies that the holder of a Call will not wish to exercise his option until the expiration date of the contract, if at all. Consequently, it is reasonable to argue that such an assumption, when applied to stock options, is in close accordance both with the actual practices of option traders and with some theoretical models of the value of certain options. It is also clear that, in order to compare option strategies with other market strategies, one must impose the same holding period and the same prohibition against interim trading for all strategies.

Nevertheless, it seemed desirable to perform at least one set of experiments in which interim trading is not prohibited. Clearly, a new set of difficulties arises when one permits interim trading, since one could make many alternative assumptions about the criteria that might govern such trading. Since a completely general formulation of this problem would have involved us in a dynamic programming problem of formidable complexity, we contented ourselves with restricting the nature of interim trading in the following way: (1) interim trades occur (if at all) only at the mid point of the 190-day period; (2) they are undertaken only for the purpose of minimizing

---

[2] SEC, *Put and Call Options*, p. 51. Of course, despite the fact that the Call option was exercised on the expiration date, the option holder may still have engaged in some trading against the option during the option period. Through interviews, however, the SEC learned that most buyers of options did not engage in any trading on the stock in question during the option period.

[3] Actually, as will be explained later, the option buyer has to sell his option to a third party after a six-month holding period in order to obtain favorable capital-gains treatment.

losses. A full description and analysis of these experiments is contained in Section 5.4.

2.3
The Sixteen Strategies

The sixteen investment strategies assumed to be available to the representative investor will be described in detail.[4] Illustrative calculations will be made for several strategies so that the reader may see exactly how the payoff numbers are calculated. As indicated earlier, it is assumed that the typical common stock sells at fifty dollars per share at the beginning of the holding period. For the moment, it is further assumed that, at the end of the holding period, nature draws from its urn a stock price within a range of plus or minus ten points from the opening price. The investor then closes out whatever position he has and his payoff is calculated.

2.3.1 Strategy 1. Cash

In Strategy 1, Cash, several alternative strategies utilizing different types of debt instruments are combined. It is assumed that an investor who wished to hold cash would invest in 190-day Treasury bills and let them mature. The yield received by the investor was estimated to be $3\frac{1}{4}$ per cent (an average bill rate during the 1960–1964 period). The gain ratio (the investor's gains per dollar of investment) is equal to 0.01715, and it is independent of future common-stock values.[5] The investor has no "position," that is, he has no stake in any market price changes.[6] The horizontal line marked c (for Cash) in Figure 2-1 indicates that stock price changes make no difference to the investor who uses this strategy.

---

[4] In this discussion it is convenient to make use of the expository techniques developed by Richard Kruizenga in "An Introduction to the Option Contract," in Cootner, ed., *Stock Market Prices,* pp. 377–391.

[5] The gain ratio is calculated as follows: for every dollar of investment the investor receives $\left\{ \dfrac{190 \text{ days}}{360 \text{ days}} \right\} \times (0.0325) = 0.01715.$

[6] It may be argued that the investor suffers an opportunity loss if the market price of common shares rises during the period. However, were one to make such an opportunity-cost calculation one would not be able to distinguish a zero position from the basic long and short positions that are described in Sections 2.3.2 and 2.3.3:

2.3.2 Strategy 2. Buy Stock

Strategy 2 entails the round-lot purchase of stock at a current market price of $50. The initial investment is considered to be the purchase price of the stock plus the standard New York Stock Exchange commission. At the end of the 190-day holding period, the investor is assumed to dispose of his holdings at the then prevailing market prices, which may be higher or lower than the initial purchase price. His sales proceeds are calculated from the assumed terminal market price minus relevant commissions, transfer taxes, and SEC fees. The net sales proceeds minus the total purchase cost per dollar of investment is the relevant gain ratio calculated. The gains, of course, depend directly upon the price change of the common stock.

An investor undertaking Strategy 2 is said to be in a long position. The investor with a long position benefits to the extent that the market price of the stock rises, and he loses to the extent the market price declines. The relevant payoff values as a function of stock price changes are shown on Figure 2-1 by the line labeled BS (Buy Stock).

2.3.3 Strategy 3. Sell Stock (Short)

In Strategy 3 the investor sells short (round lots of) stock. In a short sale an investor sells stock he does not own in the hope of purchasing it back later at a lower price. The short seller delivers the stock he has sold to the buyer by borrowing it from a broker. When the seller finally "covers" his short position (by buying the common stock at a later date), he returns the borrowed stock. In this strategy the investor is assumed to deposit an amount of cash with his broker equal to the full proceeds from the short sale. This represents his initial investment for the short position. The gain ratio is calculated in precisely the same way as for Strategy 2.[7] This position is called a basic short position. The investor (speculator) benefits to the extent that the price declines, and he loses when the market price advances. Payoff values are shown in Figure 2-1. Note that by ignoring opportunity-cost considerations, the cash position (Strategy 1, the zero

---

[7] We shall defer for the moment an actual example of the calculation involving stock exchange commissions and various fees.

position) is contrasted with both the basic long position (Strategy 2) and the basic short position (Strategy 3).

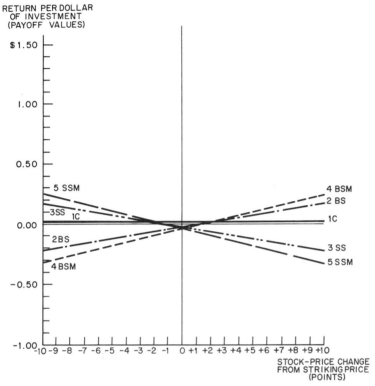

Figure 2-1
Trading positions for strategies involving the buying and selling of stock and holding cash. All strategies other than cash intersect the zero price-change line at a negative payoff value because of transactions costs.

2.3.4 Strategies 4 and 5. Buy Stock on Margin;
Sell Stock (Short) on Margin

These strategies are identical to Strategies 2 and 3 with respect to the long and short positions but differ with respect to the leverage involved. In the margin strategies, the investor does not put up the full amount of money required for the transaction. Rather he puts

41

up a certain percentage of the total amount (the margin) which is assumed to be not less than 70 per cent. The minimum margin requirement is employed in the calculations. The remaining 30 per cent is borrowed from the broker at an interest rate that is assumed to be 5 per cent. This rate represents an average rate charged margin borrowers during the 1960–1964 period. In buying stock on margin, the gains before interest expense are identical to those for Strategy 2 except that approximately $1.43 of stock can be bought for each dollar of investment. Payoff values for Strategies 4 and 5 are also shown on Figure 2-1 so that they may be contrasted with those for Strategies 2 and 3. It is worth noting that the short and long strategies imply negative returns for a zero price change because of transactions costs.

2.3.5 Strategy 6. Buy Call

In this strategy the investor buys a Call option, an option to purchase 100 shares of common stock at the fixed price of $50 per share (called the option price) any time within the next 190 days.[8] It is assumed that the cost of this contract to the option buyer is $587.50. This figure is considered to be a typical price of a 190-day Call option for 100 shares of a $50 stock during the 1960–1964 period.[9] We assume that the option buyer makes a decision whether or not to exercise his option on the last day of the option period. If the market price does not rise sufficiently above the option price to cover the transactions costs (as would be the case, for example, if the market price of the common stock was $50 or less at the end of the option period), the investor will not exercise the Call and will lose 100 per cent of his investment. His gain ratio is then −1.00. If the future market price exceeds the option price by more than the transactions cost, the investor will exercise the Call. He will simul-

---

[8] The option price need not be the current market price, but in practice the two prices are usually the same. The option price is reduced during the option period to the extent of any dividend payments made on the stock. The adjusted option price is referred to as the striking price of the option. See Section 2.4 for a fuller discussion of dividends. Throughout Section 2.3, however, we assume no dividends are paid and thus the option price and the striking price are identical.

[9] This and other option-cost figures were estimated by the option dealers interviewed in the course of this study. The estimates were then checked against records of actual option transactions.

taneously purchase 100 shares of common stock at the striking price of $50, plus commission, from the option writer and then sell the shares on the open market at the going market price less commissions, taxes, and SEC fees.[10] This final sale is required by Assumption 7 stipulating that the investor end with a portfolio consisting entirely of cash. His profit will be the excess of the net proceeds of the sale over the sum of the premium and his total cost of acquiring the stock. A typical calculation of the gain ratio from buying a Call option is illustrated below. Assume that the common stock sells at $60 at the end of the option period. The calculation of the gain ratio proceeds as follows:

Proceeds from Sale of Shares on Open Market:[11]	100 Shares at $60.00 per share		$6000.00
	Less: brokerage fee	45.00	
	federal transfer tax	2.40	
	New York transfer tax	4.00	
	SEC fee	.12	
	Total commissions and taxes based on 1960– 1964 rates	51.52	
	Net proceeds		**5948.48**
Cost of Calling Shares at the Striking Price:	100 Shares at $50.00 per share		5000.00
	plus brokerage fee		44.00
	Total cost of shares optioned		5044.00
	plus option premium		587.50
	Total cost		**5631.50**

The gain ratio may now be calculated from equation (2.1) as follows:

$$\text{Gain ratio} = \frac{\text{Net proceeds} - \text{total cost}}{\text{Initial investment}} \qquad (2.1)$$

$$= \frac{(\$5948.48 - \$5631.50)}{\$587.50} = 0.5395$$

Note that total transactions costs (brokerage fees on both the buying and selling side plus taxes and fees) are far from insignificant. They

---

[10] In all calculations performed for this study a charge for the federal transfer tax was included. This tax was in effect during the 1960–1964 period, but security transactions have not been subject to federal transfer taxes since December 31, 1965. Nevertheless, the New York transfer tax has been raised since 1964, and consequently the calculations above are still approximately correct for present conditions.

[11] Taxes and the SEC fee are charged only to the seller of shares.

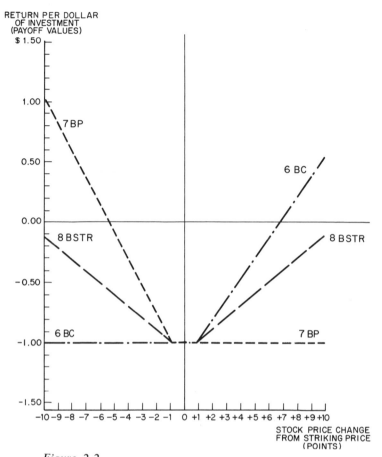

Figure 2-2

Trading positions for option buyers, representing Strategies 6, 7, and 8. The kinks near the zero price-change line reflect the fact that Calls and Puts are not exercised until there has been sufficient price movement to cover the transactions costs of exercising the options.

amount to more than 16 per cent of the initial investment. The returns to this and the next two strategies are represented in Figure 2-2. The present strategy is depicted by the line BC (Buy Call).

2.3.6 Strategy 7. Buy Put

The seventh strategy available to the investor is the purchase of a Put option. A Put option gives the holder the privilege to sell 100

44

shares of stock to the option writer at the option price (assumed to be the current market price of $50) at any time within the next six months and ten days. A typical Put option of this duration on a $50 stock is assumed to cost $450. If the market price is $50 or above at the end of the option period, the option will not be exercised and the buyer will lose his initial investment (that is, his gain ratio is −1.00). If the option is exercised, the option buyer simultaneously sells the stock to the option writer at the $50 striking price (less commission, taxes, and SEC fee) and buys the stock at the current market price plus commission. Gain ratios for Put and Call buying are shown in Figure 2-2. Note that the two strategies of buying Put and Call options are much more highly leveraged than the preceding five strategies. That is to say, percentage gain and loss ratios are far larger for these strategies than for any of the earlier ones. This is shown in Figure 2-2 by the far steeper slopes of the Call and Put curves which, while they leave one vulnerable to loss for much of the relevant range of stock prices, also rise rapidly to high payoff levels.

The attractiveness of Put and Call options lies in the opportunity they afford for investing a small amount of capital.[12] The buyer's motivation might be captured in the following example. An individual believes that the common stock of Ford Motor Company, currently selling at $50 per share, is likely to appreciate substantially over the next six months. He knows, however, that the security has tended to fluctuate widely and could be subject to large downward movements. He buys a Call option, good for six months and ten days, for a premium of, say, $587.50. If he is correct in his judgment and the common stock rises to, say, $80 by the end of the option period, he will earn a profit of $2314.14.[13] If he is wrong, however, and the common falls to $20 per share, the individual loses the entire $587.50 option premium.

---

[12] See SEC, *Put and Call Options,* pp. 76–77, which also suggests that most Call-option buyers immediately dispose of any stock acquired upon the exercise of the option, i.e., that many investors actually behave in accordance with the assumptions of this "cash-to-cash" case.

[13] The profit is calculated as follows: Net profit equals $3000 (100 shares × $30 per share appreciation) less $98.36 (brokerage charges and taxes) and also minus $587.50 (the option premium). Moreover, as we shall see later in this chapter, this gain can be established as a long-term capital gain while, through an appropriate strategy, the losses may be taken as short-term capital losses. See Section 2.5.2.

2.3.7 Strategy 8. Buy Straddle

A Straddle is a combination of one Put and one Call option on the same stock, at the same option price, and with the same expiration date. The Put half of the Straddle gives the holder the right, at any time during the option period, to sell the writer of the contract the stated number of shares of the stock at the option price. The Call option gives the Straddle buyer the right to buy from the option writer the stated number of shares of the stock at the same price. The exercise of one contract before expiration does *not* void the remaining option.

The Straddle buyer benefits to the extent the market price rises above and/or falls below the striking price by at least enough to cover the transactions costs involved in exercising the profitable side of the Straddle. His actual dollar gains and losses are shown in Figure 2-2, where they are contrasted with the trading positions of the simple Put and Call buyer. The kinks in the figure at prices plus and minus one point reflect the fact that it just becomes profitable to exercise Call and Put options, respectively, at these prices. Similar kinks will also be seen in the tables that follow.

2.3.8 Vector Notation of the Investor's Position

It will be useful to discuss at this point the simple vector notation that was introduced in 2.1. It serves as a heuristic device to determine an investor's net position and will prove particularly convenient in ascertaining an investor's interests when we deal with combinations of basic strategies. The device was first used by Richard Kruizenga who in turn credits Paul Samuelson with originating the idea.[14]

An investor's position is described by a two-element column vector. The first element in the vector indicates how an investor is affected by an upward movement in the price of the common stock. If that element is unity, the investor benefits from upward price movements; if the element is −1 the investor loses by any upward price movements. If the element is zero the investor is unaffected by

---

[14] See Richard Kruizenga, "An Introduction to the Option Contract," in Cootner ed., *Stock Market Prices*, pp. 387–389.

upward price movements. The second element shows how an investor fares from downward price changes. The element is $+1$ if he benefits, -1 if he loses, and 0 if he is indifferent to such price movements.

These vectors indicate gains in a crude sense and make no allowance for any premium paid for the option nor do they include such considerations as transactions costs. Thus they are not useful for making profit calculations. The advantage of the notation, however, is that as long as the basic unit of trading is the same for all positions, for example, 100-share lots, one can easily describe the investor's net trading position even if he engages in several kinds of transactions at the same time.

One can easily use these vectors to describe the trading positions of an investor who employs the first seven strategies. Strategy 1, the holding of cash, may be described by the vector $\begin{bmatrix} 0 \\ 0 \end{bmatrix}$. An investor holding cash is indifferent to both upward and downward price movements in the stock market. Strategy 2, the basic long position, may be described by the vector $\begin{bmatrix} +1 \\ -1 \end{bmatrix}$. The investor gains by upward price movements and loses if the market price declines. Strategy 3, the basic short position, is described by the vector $\begin{bmatrix} -1 \\ +1 \end{bmatrix}$. The investor loses when the stock price rises and gains from any decline. The position of an individual who buys a Call option (Strategy 6) may be represented by the vector $\begin{bmatrix} +1 \\ 0 \end{bmatrix}$. The investor gains if the market price of the stock advances above the striking price and is indifferent to any declines. This is so because the investor loses the premium paid for the Call option whether the market price has declined by one point or by 10 points. The position of the buyer of a Put option may be represented by the $\begin{bmatrix} 0 \\ +1 \end{bmatrix}$ vector. He is indifferent to price rises whereas he gains to the extent that the market price declines from the striking price. The buyer of a Straddle benefits from both upward and downward price movements, and therefore his position is represented by the $\begin{bmatrix} +1 \\ +1 \end{bmatrix}$ vector.

This vector notation will be convenient in explaining the phenomenon of option conversion. Most buyers of stock options tend to be bullish about the prospects for the stock market, and consequently they prefer, other things being equal, to buy Call rather than Put options. By the same argument one would expect option writers to prefer to issue Puts rather than Calls. In fact, many option writers prefer to write Straddles, since the writer of a Straddle (one Put plus one Call) need put up neither more margin nor more securities than would be required to write a Call option alone, whereas the Straddle premium is, of course, substantially larger than the premium for a simple Call. Many Puts are initially issued by writers of Straddles. These arguments suggest that if Puts and Calls were equally costly, there would tend to be an excess supply of Puts. Option buyers would demand more Calls than Puts while option issuers would have the opposite supply propensities. Consequently, Call options are higher priced than Put options. The possibility of option conversion, however, limits the spread between the premiums of Put and Call options.

As was indicated in Chapter 1, a conversion of a Put to a Call option can be accomplished by a financial intermediary in the following manner: the intermediary simultaneously buys a Put, buys 100 shares of the common stock, and writes (issues) a Call. By so doing the converter assumes no risk. He is unaffected by any possible price movements, as is shown by this vector representation:

$$\begin{bmatrix} 0 \\ +1 \end{bmatrix} + \begin{bmatrix} +1 \\ -1 \end{bmatrix} + \begin{bmatrix} -1 \\ 0 \end{bmatrix} = \begin{bmatrix} 0 \\ 0 \end{bmatrix}$$

Buy	Buy	Sell	Converter's
Put	Stock	Call	Net Position

The converter's net position may be found by simple vector addition. Moreover, this technique applies quite generally to any set of compound positions: by adding the corresponding vectors one can determine the net position of the investor.

The Securities and Exchange Commission found that of the 217,400 shares of Puts originally written during June of 1959, 171,550 shares, or 79 per cent, were converted to Calls.[15] Such conversions set a spread between Put and Call options. If, for example, an increase in the demand for Call options tended to drive up the

---

[15] SEC, *Put and Call Options*, p. 31.

Call premium, the action of converters would raise the demand for Puts and also the supply of Calls, thus tending to restore the original price difference.[16] We have assumed that the difference between Put and Call premiums is $137.50. This difference was considered typical of the period from 1960 to 1964.

2.3.9 Strategies 9 and 11. Writing Calls

In Strategies 9 and 11, the investor writes (sells) a Call option. The position of the writer of a Call option who does not also own the underlying stock is just the opposite of that of the buyer. If the price of the stock has not risen above the $50 striking price at the end of the contract period by enough to cover the transactions costs of the buyer, the Call will not be exercised and the writer will gain the full amount of the premium.[17] Nevertheless, the Call writer gains the full amount of the premium whether the stock price at the end of the period is $50 a share or $35 a share. Consequently, the second element of his vector is zero. On the other hand, if the stock is sufficiently above $50, the Call will be exercised and the writer will have to buy stock to meet the Call. The return from the premium he has received will be reduced by the difference between the market price and the striking price, plus two stock exchange commissions and other expenses.[18] But in Strategy 9 the investor also simultaneously buys 100 shares of common stock. Thus, he is protected from the unlimited potential capital loss that is involved in writing a Call option without owning the stock. Indeed, the investor who undertakes Strategy 9 is unaffected by the extent to which the common stock rises. If the option is exercised, he simply sells the shares he owns at the striking price. His proceeds consist of the striking price times the number of shares optioned plus the option premium and less transactions costs. In vector notation his position is as follows:

---

[16] This assumes that the original spread between the Put and Call premiums was such as to induce converters to enter the market.

[17] Writers of Calls on a typical $50 stock receive $525, $62.50 less than the $587.50 assumed cost of the Call option to the buyer. The difference (spread) is made up of middlemen's commissions and is considered typical of the 1960–1964 period. It should be pointed out that some option brokers have claimed that they are able to operate on a slightly smaller spread.

[18] As will be explained later, for tax purposes the sales price of the shares is increased by the amount of the Call premium.

$$\begin{bmatrix} +1 \\ -1 \end{bmatrix} + \begin{bmatrix} -1 \\ 0 \end{bmatrix} = \begin{bmatrix} 0 \\ -1 \end{bmatrix}$$

Buy	Sell	Net Position of Individual
Stock	Call	Undertaking Strategy 9

While the investor loses from downward price movements, as is indicated by the bottom element of the vector, he does not suffer a net loss unless the price declines by an amount exceeding the Call premium (net of commissions).

A second, more daring, strategy available to the option writer is to write a Call option without the protection of owning the com-

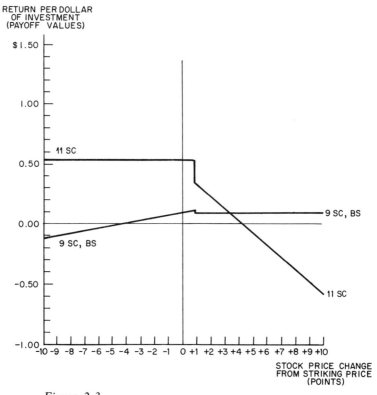

Figure 2-3

Trading positions for sellers of Calls. The discontinuities in the diagram reflect the fact that Call options are not exercised until the market price has risen sufficiently to cover the transaction costs involved in exercising them.

mon stock (Strategy 11). In this case the writer simply deposits 30 per cent of the value of the stock optioned.[19] If the stock is called at the end of the option period, the writer is required to purchase the stock at that future market price and sell the shares to the option buyer at the striking price. This profit or loss will be the proceeds of the sale plus the premium minus the cost of the purchase. Figure 2-3 depicts the difference in the actual payoffs accruing to option writers using Strategies 9 and 11 for alternative terminal values of the common stock.

2.3.10 Strategies 10 and 12. Writing Puts

Strategies 10 and 12 are the converse of Strategies 9 and 11. They cover the cases of writing Puts while either owning the stock or with no position in the stock, respectively. First consider the position of the Put option writer who has no position in the common stock. In this case the option writer is required to put up an initial margin of at least 25 per cent of the market value of the stock upon which the Put has been written.[20] The procedure in writing a Put on a $50

---

[19] It should be noted that 30 per cent was the minimum margin requirement on such a transaction during the 1960–1964 period. Some brokerage firms insist on a larger margin than the minimum requirement. If a broker allows an option writer to put up the minimum margin, however, the out-of-pocket amount of cash he has to put up himself is actually less than 30 per cent of the market value of the stock. This is so because the premium paid to the option writer may be used to cover part of his margin requirement. Thus the margin requirement on writing a Call option on a 100-share lot of a $50 stock is $1500 (30 per cent of $5000). Nevertheless, since he received $525 for writing the option, he must only put up $975.

[20] Again we emphasize that 25 per cent was a *minimum* margin requirement for writing Put options during the 1960–1964 period. In Strategy 12 it is assumed that the individual deposits with his broker only the minimum margin required. However, there is also a maintenance margin requirement. This means that if the common stock declines during the option period, the Put writer will be required to deposit additional margin. In the calculations of the investor's investment, however, the additional margin that may be required has been ignored. This rule of thumb has been chosen because it seemed impossible to specify the investor's actual average investment without knowing the market price of the common stock throughout every day of the option period. Of course, it is also true that if the market price of the common rises, the investor may be able to take out some of the initial capital he was required to put up under the initial margin requirement. Thus, the actual investment of the Put writer may in fact turn out to be less than had been assumed. In essence then, the practice of ignoring any additional investment that may have to be made implicitly assumes that for the typical option writer the additional margin he is required to put up is exactly balanced by the released margin that accrues to him when the market price of the common rises.

stock is as follows: the writer puts up $862.50 (25 per cent of $5000 less $387.50 assumed to be the premium that he collects).[21] If the price of the stock does not fall below the striking price by an amount sufficient to cover transactions costs (as would be the case if the market price six months and ten days after the Put was issued was $50 or above), the Put is not exercised and the writer collects the $1250 margin on deposit and realizes a profit of $387.50. If the price does fall sufficiently, however, the Put will be exercised. The writer is then obliged to buy the shares from the option buyer at the $50 striking price plus commission. The cost basis of his shares would be reduced, however, by the amount of the premium received. Under the assumption of the cash-to-cash model, he would then sell the Put shares on the open market and receive the market value of the common stock less commission and transfer taxes. His profit or loss would consist of the difference between (a) the sum of the sales proceeds and the option premium and (b) the total cost of the stock purchased at the striking price.

In Strategy 10 the investor purchases 100 shares of stock at $50 per share (plus relevant commission) and then writes a Put option. His net position may be shown by the following vector notation:

$$\begin{bmatrix} 0 \\ -1 \end{bmatrix} + \begin{bmatrix} +1 \\ -1 \end{bmatrix} = \begin{bmatrix} +1 \\ -2 \end{bmatrix}$$

Sell	Buy	Net Position of Investor
Put	Stock	Under Strategy 10

Figure 2-4 shows the actual payoff values for the two different strategies of writing Puts.[22]

---

[21] As noted earlier, the writer of an option is assumed to receive $62.50 less than the amount paid by the option buyer.

[22] The reader may wonder why we have not considered the combination strategy of selling short and buying a Put. This is a more protected position than either Strategies 9 or 11. There are several reasons why this strategy was not included. In the first place, one can think of literally hundreds of combination strategies involving stock options. It was simply impossible to consider them all. The particular combination of writing a Put and selling short is not at all a common strategy as has been revealed by a survey conducted by the Securities and Exchange Commission (see the Commission's *Report on Put and Call Options,* p. 58). Apparently, most people write Puts in stocks that they find attractive for investment and in which they wish to acquire additional shares at a lower price. Moreover, in Strategy 16 we have considered a strategy much like the one proposed. We preferred to consider Strategy 16 (selling short and buying a Call) since it is

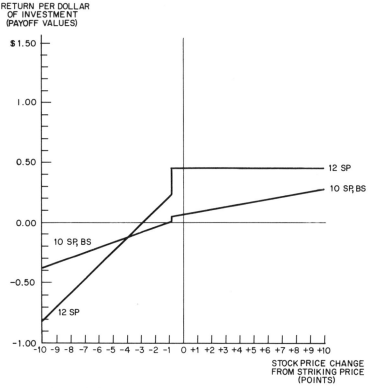

Figure 2-4
Trading positions for sellers of Puts.

2.3.11 Strategies 13 and 14. Selling Straddles

A Straddle consists of one Put and one Call option. In Strategy 13, sell Straddle, buy stock, the investor is assumed to buy a round lot of common stock and then issue one Call and one Put option on the shares. The investor's net position is the same as it would be if he sold two Puts (ignoring differences in option premiums and brokerage charges). This can be shown easily in terms of our vector notation.

---

highly recommended by many of the option dealers. See, for example, Herbert Filer, *Put and Call Options*, p. 64. Since one of the purposes of our study was to examine the rationality of option strategies suggested by option dealers and utilized in the market, it seemed that this was a more reasonable strategy to consider.

$$\begin{bmatrix} -1 \\ 0 \end{bmatrix} + \begin{bmatrix} 0 \\ -1 \end{bmatrix} + \begin{bmatrix} +1 \\ -1 \end{bmatrix} = \qquad \begin{bmatrix} 0 \\ -2 \end{bmatrix}$$

Sell	Sell	Buy	Net Position of Investor
Call	Put	Stock	Under Strategy 13

In Strategy 14, sell Straddle, the investor has no position in the stock and puts up 30 per cent margin (the minimum margin require-

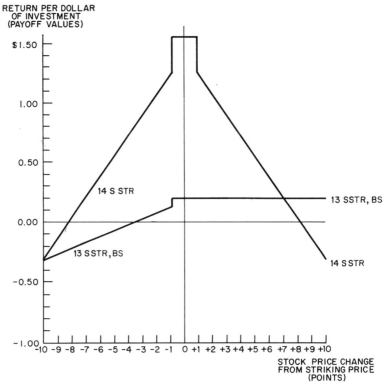

RETURN PER DOLLAR
OF INVESTMENT
(PAYOFF VALUES)

STOCK PRICE CHANGE
FROM STRIKING PRICE
(POINTS)

Figure 2-5
Trading positions for sellers of Straddles.

ment during the 1960–1964 period was the same as that for a Call) to secure his position. The relevant payoff values are displayed in Figure 2-5.[23]

---

[23] The payoff values assume that the option either remains unexercised at the end of the contract period or that either side of the option is exercised. It is, of course, possible in practice that both sides of a Straddle are exercised. For example,

*2.3.12   Strategies 15 and 16.   Combining Basic Long
and Short Positions with Option Buying*

Strategy 15, buy stock, buy Put, involves the purchase of a Put option to protect a long position. This case is an important one because of the emphasis placed in the literature on the insurance value afforded by the purchase of options as opposed to their speculative use.[24] The following represents the typical example given to explain the motivation for such a strategy.

An investor buys 100 shares of Ford at $50. He is convinced that the stock will go up but wishes to protect himself in case his judgment is wrong. Consequently, at the same time he buys a Put option good for six months and ten days. The Put allows him to carry the stock fully protected for the duration of the option. If the price declines he cannot lose more than $450, the cost of the option (plus commissions and expenses), because he will be able to exercise his Put at the striking price of $50 per share. On the other hand, if the common stock does rise as he expects, his option has become worthless but he can sell his stock at the (higher) market price. In calculating his returns, the investor adds the $450 premium to the cost price of the shares. The investor's net position can be shown in terms of vector notation:

$$\begin{bmatrix} +1 \\ -1 \end{bmatrix} + \begin{bmatrix} 0 \\ +1 \end{bmatrix} = \begin{bmatrix} +1 \\ 0 \end{bmatrix}$$

Buy	Buy	Net Position of Investor
Stock	Put	Under Strategy 15

Strategy 16, sell stock, buy Call, involves the short sale of common stock and the simultaneous purchase of a Call option. Again an illustration will help explain the possible motivation for such a strategy. Assume that an investor feels that Ford, now selling at $50, will in fact decline; therefore he sells 100 shares short. Nevertheless,

---

if the stock price first rises the Call might be exercised. Later the price could fall below the striking price and the Put could be exercised. We have ruled out this possibility by our assumption that no action is taken until the end of the contract period.

[24] See, for example, Filer, *Put and Call Options,* pp. 52–54.

he is not willing to risk an unlimited loss if his judgment proves wrong and the market price of the common advances. So he buys a Call option at $50, good for six months and ten days, for which he pays a premium of $587.50. He is now guaranteed that, should his judgment prove wrong, he can buy 100 shares of common at $50 and his loss will be limited to the cost of his Call option plus expenses. On the other hand, if the investor was right in his initial judgment and the stock did decline, his Call option has become

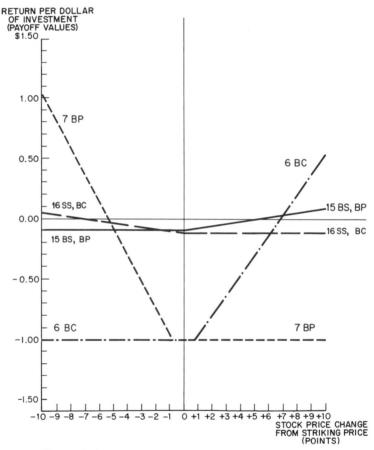

Figure 2-6

Trading positions for combination strategies involving option buying. For comparison, the basic buy-Put and buy-Call payoffs are also shown.

worthless, but he has gained from the short sale. In terms of the vector notation the investor's net position is:

$$
\begin{bmatrix} -1 \\ +1 \end{bmatrix} + \begin{bmatrix} +1 \\ 0 \end{bmatrix} = \begin{bmatrix} 0 \\ +1 \end{bmatrix}
$$

Sell Stock   Buy Call   Net Position of Investor
Short   Under Strategy 16

The payoffs for Strategies 15 and 16 are graphed in Figure 2-6, where the returns from simple Put and Call buying strategies are also shown for comparison.

2.3.13 Recapitulation

It is clear that the sixteen basic strategies assumed to be available to the representative investor form only a partial list of the available alternatives. For example, the investor might buy convertible bonds, warrants, real estate, or even art objects. An infinite number of pure and combination strategies could be added. Nevertheless, a model has to be simple to be tractable.[25] As it is, the present model goes a long way toward integrating option trading into general portfolio behavior and is a much richer model of security choice and option dealing than other current models.

Despite the large number of possibilities we have offered our representative investor, we have consciously eliminated several interesting alternatives. For example, we do not let the investor liquidate his position prior to the end of his horizon period. Nor do we let him change his position in the middle of the holding period upon receipt of new information or in response to a swing in the market price of the stock. For example, an investor may have purchased a Put option. The next month the price of the common declines by ten points. Perhaps the investor would like to buy the stock since he has a guaranteed buyer at the striking price ten points higher. Although the SEC in its study found little evidence of such trading, it would be desirable to consider some of these strategies in a study of optimal behavior. Some of the dynamic problems in choosing optimal option strategies are treated in Section 5.4.

---

[25] One might also add that convertibles and warrants are available on only a few securities, whereas options can be bought and sold on almost all actively traded issues.

2.4
The Effect of Dividend Payments
on the Sixteen Strategies

Thus far dividend payments have been ignored in the calculation of the payoffs from the sixteen alternative investment strategies. The neglect of dividend payments would make no difference if the inclusion affected all strategies equally. In practice, however, the payment of dividends tends to favor some of the strategies. Consequently, it seemed necessary to examine the case where the representative stock is assumed to pay a dividend during the 190-day holding period.

Assume that the typical $50 stock pays a $1 dividend during the holding period. Investors who have a long position in the stock are, of course, entitled to receive the dividend. Investors who have a short position in the stock, however, are required to pay the dividend to the owner of the stock they have borrowed.[26] The effect of dividend payments on Put and Call options is only slightly more complicated. On a day when a stock sells ex-dividend (that is, the day following the date when all owners of the security are entitled to receive a cash dividend) the option prices of all existing Put and Call options on that stock will automatically be reduced by the amount of the dividend. For example, the holder of either a Put or a Call option at a contract (option) price of $50 will automatically reduce the option price of the option to $49 on the ex-dividend date. As noted earlier, the option price as adjusted for dividends paid during the contract period is called the striking price of the option. Thus while the actual holder of the stock would receive the dividend on the date it is payable, the holder of a Call option does not receive the dividend but rather reduces the option price of his Call. If he

---

[26] Recall that when an individual sells short he must borrow the securities from some other stockholder in order to be able to deliver the shares to the buyer. However, the lender of stock is entitled to receive any dividends declared thereon. Similarly, the individual who bought the stock from the short seller is also entitled to receive the dividends. The registered owner of the security (the buyer of the stock from the short seller) will receive his dividend directly from the company. The lender of the stock, on the other hand, looks to the short seller (who has borrowed the stock) for his dividend.

later exercises his Call option, the effect on his dollar return will be the same as it would have been if he had been paid the dividend in the first place.[27] However, if the price of the stock is below $49 (the contract price minus the dividend) on the expiration date of the option, the holder of the Call option will not exercise his option and will not receive the dividend.

Similarly, the short seller of stock is always charged for a dividend, while the holder of a Put contract reduces the option price of his contract and therefore pays the dividend if and only if he exercises the option. Table 2-2 shows the effect of these general rules on each of the sixteen strategies available to the investor. In making up the table, it was assumed that a dividend of less than $0.95 is paid during the 190-day option period. If a larger dividend were paid, the prices in the table would not be the same.[28]

2.5
The Effect of Personal Income Taxes on the Sixteen Strategies

If the tax consequences of profits and losses from option transactions and from transactions involving the buying and selling of common shares were identical, tax considerations would not alter the relative attractiveness of the various strategies.[29] In practice, however, the tax laws do not have the same effect on all our strategies.[30] Specifically, present tax laws permit option buyers certain advantages that cannot be gained by taking positions directly in the common stock. Moreover, in certain cases option buyers may be treated more

---

[27] For tax purposes, however, the dividend becomes a capital gain rather than income.

[28] For example, assume a $2.50 dividend is paid during the 190-day period. In that case, it will pay the Call buyer (Strategy 6) to exercise his Call if the price is $49 or greater. Consequently, the entries in the last column would read: $P > 48$: + Dividend; $P \leq 48$: No change.

[29] Of course, it would still be true that tax laws that did not allow unlimited loss offset would make all strategies involving the possibility of losses less desirable than holding cash.

[30] The basic reason for this is that the income tax law accords different treatment to (a) long-term capital gains, (b) long-term capital losses, (c) short-term capital gains, (d) short-term capital losses, and (e) ordinary income and deductions. Because of these differences a given income of one class may produce more after-tax income than would be produced by a larger pre-tax income of another class.

Table 2-2

**Effect of Dividend Payments
on the Sixteen Strategies**

Strategy			Effect of Dividend Payments on Investor's Position
1	C	Cash	No change
2	BS	Buy Stock	+ Dividend
3	SS	Sell Stock (Short)	− Dividend
4	BSM	Buy Stock on Margin	+ Dividend
5	SSM	Sell Stock (Short) on Margin	− Dividend
6	BC	Buy Call	$P > 50$: + Dividend
			$P \leq 50$: No change
7	BP	Buy Put	$P \geq 50$: No change
			$P < 50$: − Dividend
8	BSTR	Buy Straddle	$P > 50$: + Dividend
			$P = 50$: No change
			$P < 50$: − Dividend
9	SC,BS	Sell (Write) Call	$P > 50$: No change
		Buy Stock	$P \leq 50$: + Dividend
10	SP,BS	Sell (Write) Put	$P \geq 50$: + Dividend
		Buy Stock	$P < 50$: + 2 Dividends
11	SC	Sell Call	$P > 50$: − Dividend
			$P \leq 50$: No change
12	SP	Sell Put	$P \geq 50$: No change
			$P < 50$: + Dividend
13	SSTR,BS	Sell Straddle (Call and Put)	$P > 50$: No change
		Buy Stock	$P = 50$: + Dividend
			$P < 50$: + 2 Dividends
14	SSTR	Sell Straddle	$P > 50$: − Dividend
			$P = 50$: No change
			$P < 50$: + Dividend
15	BS,BP	Buy Stock	$P \geq 50$: + Dividend
		Buy Put	$P < 50$: No change
16	SS,BC	Sell Stock	$P > 50$: No change
		Buy Call	$P \leq 50$: − Dividend

favorably for tax purposes than option writers. Thus tax considerations will not only change the relative attractiveness of option strategies vis-à-vis taking positions directly in common shares but will also affect the relative attractiveness of writing versus buying options.

2.5.1 General Tax Consequences of Option Transactions

Before we describe the provisions of the tax laws affecting options, a caveat is in order. The tax status of option transactions is not always unambiguous. Option dealers interviewed during the course of this study have indicated that Internal Revenue investigators have not always been consistent in applying the tax laws. Consequently, the reader is cautioned that the tax treatment described here is not meant to be an authoritative guide to the appropriate method of reporting the profits from option transactions on individual income tax returns. Nevertheless, it seems fair to say that the tax treatment described below is widely understood by option traders to be acceptable under current income tax regulations. The tax treatment of options described in this section is generally consistent with the treatment recommended in two widely used tax guides.[31] These guides have served as popular references to the tax treatment of the income from Puts and Calls and thus have influenced the behavior of individual buyers and sellers.

2.5.2 Tax Treatment of Returns from Buying Puts and Calls

The major advantage of Put and Call options is that they may be treated as capital assets for tax purposes. Thus if the Put or Call buyer sells an option that he has purchased, the difference between the purchase price and the sale price of the option is treated as a capital gain or loss. This gain or loss is designated as "long term" if the individual held the option for over six months. Otherwise the gain or loss is treated as "short term." [32]

This provision may enable the option holder to derive significant tax advantages. Assume that an individual purchases a six-month one-day[33] Put option on 100 shares of XYZ Corporation at $50 a

---

[31] See John D. Cunnion, *How To Get Maximum Leverage from Puts and Calls* (Larchmont: Business Reports, Inc., 1966); and also Hermann Schneider and Warren Wintrub, *Tax Savings Opportunities in Securities Transactions* (New York: Lybrand, Ross Bros. & Montgomery, 1966). Earlier editions of the former guide were available to investors during the 1960–1964 period.

[32] 1954 Internal Revenue Code: Section 1234, (a) and (b).

[33] It simplifies the illustrations to assume that the option period is six months and one day rather than six months and ten days as is in fact the case.

share and has no other position in the shares. Consider first the case where the common stock price moves to $70 a share by the end of six months — that is, the option has become worthless. If the option holder simply lets his option expire, he will suffer a capital loss on the day the Put option expires. Since he held the option for (one day) more than six months, the loss would be considered long-term. Let us further assume that the individual is in the 50 per cent marginal tax bracket and that he has realized long-term and short-term gains during the year, both of which exceed the amount of the option premium. Clearly it will be to his advantage to establish the capital loss on the Put option as a short-term capital loss, for in this case he could deduct the loss in its entirety against short-term capital gains that would otherwise be taxed at normal (50 per cent) marginal income tax rates.[34] The tax laws allow him to establish this loss as a short-term capital loss by the following procedure. Just before the expiration of the six-months holding period he may arrange to sell his (currently worthless) option to a third party for the nominal price of $1. (Option dealers customarily purchase such options for their customers.) Having sold his option before the six-months holding period has past, he is now entitled to deduct the full amount of the option premium (less $1) as a *short-term* capital loss. Since his other short-term gains would have been taxed at the 50 per cent tax rate, this individual has, in effect, an out-of-pocket loss of only 50 cents on the dollar from his option transaction.[35]

Now consider the case in which the common stock falls from $50 to $30 by the end of the option period. In this case the Put option is obviously profitable. However, the individual must take care not to exercise the option. If he buys the stock in the open market at $30 a share and immediately exercises the option by

---

[34] On the other hand, if the capital loss were long-term it would have to be used to offset other long-term gains, which otherwise would be taxed at a favorable 25 per cent rate. Thus, if the investor could establish the loss as a short-term loss and if he had other short-term gains against which the loss could be written off, he would obtain a tax benefit amounting to 25 cents per dollar of loss.

[35] In order to take maximum advantage of the tax laws, the investor may have to close out his position prior to the end of the six-month ten-day period. This is a violation of our previous assumption that positions are closed out on the last day. However, it is only a minor violation which we believe is justified by the significant effect it has on the relative desirability of strategies for the taxable investor.

"Putting" the stock to the option writer at $50 a share, his gain from such a transaction will be treated as a short-term capital gain, for the stock is, in effect, bought and sold on the same day. There is a stratagem, however, that enables the option buyer to establish his capital gain as long-term. Instead of exercising the option, after a six-months holding period he can sell the option to a third party for its true market value, that is, the return after transactions costs that can be made from exercising the option. Thus, the basic tax advantage of the over-six-months (Put) option is that any profits therefrom may be established as favorably taxed long-term capital gains, while losses may be established as short-term capital losses, which may be deductible against more highly taxed short-term capital gains.[36]

Note that this favorable tax treatment is not afforded the individual who sells stock short. Under present income-tax laws, profits from short sales are considered short-term capital gains no matter how long the short position remains open. Consequently, a Put option is the only way of turning profits from a short position into long-term capital gains.

The treatment of Call options is fully analogous to the treatment of Puts. By utilizing an optimal tax strategy, the Call buyer is able to establish profits as long-term gains and losses as short-term capital losses.

2.5.3 Tax Treatment of Returns from Writing Puts and Calls

In general, the tax consequences for the option writer are not as favorable as those for the option buyer. If the option expires unexercised, the premium received by the option writer becomes ordi-

---

[36] Short-term losses are applied first against short-term gains; a net short-term loss (i.e., excess of short-term losses over short-term gains) is applied against net long-term gains. If net short-term losses for the taxable year exceed net long-term gains for the year the excess is deductible against ordinary income, but only to the extent of $1000; the remainder of the excess becomes a short-term capital loss carry-over to succeeding years. It is because of these restrictions on deduction of short-term capital losses that we have assumed that the investor has other short-term capital gains in an amount sufficient to absorb the short-term capital losses arising in his option transactions.

nary income.[37] Such ordinary income will then be subject to personal income taxes at the relevant marginal tax rate.

The situation is somewhat different if the option is exercised. If a Put option is exercised, the premium that the writer receives is deducted from the cost basis of the stock he is required to buy. If, as is required by our strategies in the cash-to-cash case, the option writer immediately sells the stock that was put to him, any capital gain or loss that results will be short term.

If a Call option is exercised, the premium that the writer receives is added to the sales price of the stock he is obliged to deliver. If such stock has been held by the writer for a period exceeding six months, any gain or loss on the sale is long-term. Consequently, if the writer purchases stock and simultaneously writes a Call option (Strategy 9) and the Call is not exercised until he has held the stock for more than six months, the writer's gain will be long term.[38]

In practice, however, the writer of a Call option that has been exercised may obtain even more favorable tax treatment. Since the technique that permits this favorable treatment is not found in the tax guides, it will be especially useful to explain the operation in detail. All transactions costs are ignored in the following illustration.

Assume an individual has bought 100 shares of XYZ Company at $50 per share and simultaneously has written a 100-share Call option at the same price (Strategy 9) for a $500 premium. Assume that at the end of the 190-day option period the market price of XYZ is $70 and the writer anticipates that the Call will be exercised. Instead of delivering the shares he already owns and realizing a $500 long-term capital gain, the option writer may employ the following technique. The option writer may buy 100 shares of XYZ at the market price of $70 and deliver these shares at $50 in fulfillment of his option contract. This produces a short-term capital loss of $1500, since the $500 premium must be added to the sales proceeds. He

---

[37] Internal Revenue Ruling: 58–234. There is an exception to this general ruling applicable to Straddles written after January 26, 1965 that will be described in Section 2.5.4.

[38] On the other hand, if the market price of the stock declines and it becomes evident before the expiration of the six-month period that the Call will not be exercised, the writer can sell the stock at the lower market price before six months have expired, thus creating a short-term capital loss. When the Call expires unexercised, the premium is ordinary income.

may then sell his shares, originally purchased at $50, at the current market price of $70, realizing a $2000 long-term capital gain. If the option writer has at least $1500 of realized short-term capital gains, the $1500 loss will offset gains that otherwise would be taxed at relatively high income-tax rates. On the other hand, the $2000 gain will receive relatively favorable capital-gains treatment. If the investor is in the 50 per cent tax bracket, the capital loss saves him $750 in taxes and thus costs him only $750, whereas the capital gain yields him $1500 after taxes. Thus the alternative technique produces a net after-tax return of $750. The investor retains 3/4 of the $2000 long-term capital gain, whereas in this example the $1500 short-term loss offsets the short-term gains that would otherwise bear a $750 tax. Had the option writer simply delivered the shares in his portfolio to fulfill his option contract, he would have realized a $500 long-term capital gain, of which he would have retained only $375 after taxes. In investigating the effect of personal income taxes on the relative desirability of option trading, we have assumed that the investor employs this trading technique whenever it is profitable for him to do so, as it will be whenever the tax benefits exceed the additional transactions costs.[39] This assumption is consistent with the actual practices of the most knowledgeable option writers.

2.5.4   Tax Treatment of Straddles

The tax treatment of the Straddle is slightly more complicated. Moreover, its tax status has changed in recent years. Formerly the Straddle was treated by many writers as a single option and the investor was required to allocate the entire premium received to whatever side of the option was exercised. The present Treasury ruling (since January 26, 1965) is that the premium received must be allocated to the constituent Put and Call options based upon the respective market values of the two options when the Straddle was written.[40] In cases where fixing such a value of the Put and Call sides of the option is difficult, the writer is allowed an alternative

---

[39] Our calculations also assume that, whenever this technique is used, the sale of the original stock and the purchase of the stock delivered when the Call is exercised will be at the same price. In practice there may be price differentials which could be either in favor of or against the investor.

[40] See Schneider and Wintrub, *Tax Savings Opportunities*, pp. 18–19.

65

method of allocating the costs. The issuer of the Straddle may allocate 55 per cent of the premium received to the Call and 45 per cent to the Put.[41] For instance, if the seller received $1000 for his Straddle, he could allocate $550 to the Call and $450 to the Put. Although the Internal Revenue Service did not specifically so rule, it is widely understood that the buyer of the Straddle can make a similar allocation if he exercises either or both sides of the option.[42] A further change provided that the income from the lapsed part of a Straddle is to be treated as a short-term capital gain instead of ordinary income.[43] We have chosen to employ these new rulings in treating the tax consequences of Straddle writing. While these rules were not applicable from 1960 through 1964, we were able to find no general agreement as to what existing practice was in the earlier period.

Consider first the tax consequences for the writer of a Straddle. Suppose that an individual sells a six-month ten-day Straddle on XYZ common stock at a contract price of $50 per share and that no dividends are paid during the contract period. Assume further that the individual buys XYZ common stock at $50 as is called for by Strategy 13. Imagine that the common stock is selling at $60 per share at the end of the option period.[44] In this case the Call part of the Straddle will be exercised. We shall assume the writer fulfills his obligation to the option buyer by selling the shares he owns at $50 a share. However, the writer is entitled to add $550, the value attributed to the Call part of the option, to the sales price of the shares. Consequently, he is able to realize a long-term capital gain of $550, the difference between the price he receives for the stock ($5000 + $550) and the $5000 purchase price for the stock. (All brokerage charges are ignored in this example.) However, the $450 value assigned to the Put part of the Straddle, which remained unexercised, must be treated as a short-term capital gain.

The tax treatment accorded to the buyer of the Straddle may be

---

[41] See Cunnion, *Maximum Leverage from Puts and Calls,* pp. 89–98. It should be pointed out that, once chosen, this method of allocation must be employed for all future Straddle premiums received.

[42] *Ibid.,* p. 94.

[43] 1954 Internal Revenue Code: Section 210; (c), (1).

[44] It is further assumed, as before, that neither side of the Straddle is exercised before the expiration date.

illustrated as follows. If the common stock rises to $60 per share by the end of the option period, the buyer will sell the Call part of the Straddle to a third party for $1000, the difference between the current market value of the stock and the option price. (The relevant brokerage charges are again ignored.) Thus, he realizes a long-term capital gain of $450, the difference between the sales price of the option ($1000) and $550, the portion of the cost of the Straddle applicable to the Call. On the other hand, the Put part of the option, for which the buyer paid an assigned value of $450, will be sold for $1 before the six-month holding period ends (see Section 2.5.2). Consequently, the $450 cost of the Put portion (less $1) may be deducted as a short-term capital loss.

Consider now the opposite case, in which the common-stock price falls from $50 to $40 by the end of the option period. The Put side of the Straddle will be exercised, and the writer will be required to buy 100 shares of stock at the $50 striking price. The option writer is able to reduce the cost of his stock for tax purposes by $450, the value originally attributed to the Put. Consequently, the cost of the stock for tax purposes is $45.50 per share rather than $50 per share. If he in turn sells the stock at the current market price of $40 he will have lost $5.50 per share or $550 for his 100 shares. This whole amount will be treated as a short-term capital loss. The writer may wish to close out his original position at $40 prior to the end of the six-month holding period to establish an additional short-term capital loss. On the other hand, the unexercised Call part of the option (to which a value of $550 was assigned) will be treated as a short-term capital gain from the point of view of the option writer.

From the point of view of the option buyer, the profits from the Put part of the option may be established as long-term capital gains (by selling the option to a third party as described above). The Call part of the option, which remains unexercised, can be established as a short-term capital loss if the buyer sells the option for $1 before the six-month holding period has expired.

2.5.5 Specific Tax Treatment of the Sixteen Strategies

In order to assess how the general tax consideration just described will affect the relative desirability of option trading, it is unavoidable to make certain specific (and, unfortunately, arbitrary) assumptions as to the tax status of the individual. One must, of course, be careful in drawing general conclusions from the tax experiments performed, since these results are dependent on the particular assumptions chosen. For example, if the option writer or buyer in question is a charitable (tax-exempt) institution, then clearly the relevant optimal strategies are those computed for the zero-tax case. For individuals in the highest marginal tax brackets, however, the effect of taxes upon the optimal strategies will be even more pronounced than is suggested by the computations based upon our specific assumptions.

The following specific assumptions are introduced.

1. The individual is in the 50 per cent marginal income tax bracket.

2. The individual has already realized during the tax year both short-term and long-term capital gains large enough to offset any capital losses he suffers through option dealing.[45]

3. The individual begins with a portfolio consisting entirely of cash. At the end of the holding period he will liquidate any position and convert his holdings to cash, that is, only the cash-to-cash case is being illustrated.

4. The individual will act optimally for tax purposes. This means that, where possible, he acts in such a way as to establish all losses as short-term capital losses and all gains as long-term capital gains.[46]

---

[45] If one did not assume that the individual had sufficient gains to offset any capital losses incurred, then it is possible that not all of his capital losses could be deducted against income, at least in the present year. This is so because net capital losses can be deducted against ordinary income only up to $1000 in any one year. Thus, one could not ascertain the individual's income tax liability without knowing the size of his initial investment. Of course, there are carry-forward provisions of the income tax laws, but a host of additional assumptions would have to be employed in order to be able to utilize such provisions in the calculations.

[46] We recognize that by allowing the representative investor to take some action prior to the expiration date of the option, we are violating one of our previous assumptions. However, if we assume that the options in question are six-month one-day options, it does not appear to be a serious breach of the assumption to allow our investor to take some action *one day* prior to the expiration date. In fact, however, since the standard option period is six months and ten days, we are making a slightly greater compromise than we would like. We feel this is justified, because the tax advantage of establishing losses as short-term capital losses is so substantial that knowledgeable option traders consistently take advantage of such opportunities.

On the basis of these assumptions one can now determine the specific tax consequences of each of the sixteen basic option strategies. Since the general tax rules have already been described in detail, the following table contains only summary comments concerning the tax treatment of the various strategies. A similar table could be constructed for the case in which the investor has an initial and terminal stock rather than cash position.

Table 2-3

Tax Consequences of the Sixteen Strategies in the Cash-to-Cash Case

---

1. Cash
Income from investment in Treasury bills is taxed at normal income tax rates (50 per cent).

2. Buy Stock
All gains are long-term and are taxed at 25 per cent.
All losses will be converted to short-term losses. The investor obtains a 50 per cent rebate (that is, he can offset short-term gains taxable at 50 per cent).

3. Sell Stock (Short)
All gains and losses are short-term and are taxed at a 50 per cent rate.

4. Buy Stock on Margin
All gains are long-term and are taxed at 25 per cent, but the interest cost on borrowed funds may offset ordinary income and obtain a 50 per cent rebate. Losses are treated as in 2.

5. Sell Stock (Short) on Margin
See 3.

6. Buy Call
All gains are established as long-term gains and are taxed at 25 per cent. All losses are established as short-term losses with a tax rebate at 50 per cent.

7. Buy Put
See 6.

8. Buy Straddle
A. If stock price remains unchanged, the option is not exercised and the premium is established as a short-term capital loss to be rebated at 50 per cent.
B. If the stock price rises (falls) sufficiently to make the Call (Put) part of Straddle profitable, the Call (Put) option is established as a long-term capital gain and is taxed at 25 per cent. The Put (Call) part of the Straddle is established as short-term capital loss and rebated at 50 per cent.

69

Table 2-3 (Cont.)

---

9. Sell Call, Buy Stock

A. If the stock price does not rise enough to cover transactions costs of the Call buyer, the option expires unexercised and the premium is ordinary income. The stock is sold prior to six-months holding period and the loss is short-term. Net profit (or loss) is taxed (rebated) at 50 per cent.

B. If the stock price rises sufficiently, the option is exercised. The investor chooses the more favorable of the following two alternatives:

1. The writer delivers his stock to the option buyer. Proceeds from sale of stock are increased by amount of option premium. Profit is long-term and is taxed at 25 per cent.

2. The writer buys stock at the market to fulfill the option contract and realizes a short-term loss that is rebated at 50 per cent. He then sells out his long position and realizes a long-term capital gain taxed at 25 per cent.

10. Sell Put, Buy Stock

A. If the stock price rises, the option expires unexercised. The premium is treated as income and is taxed at 50 per cent. The capital gain from sale of stock is long-term and is taxed at 25 per cent. If the stock price remains unchanged or does not fall enough to cover the option buyer's transactions costs, a short-term capital loss (including the brokerage charges and fees for buying and selling) is established and is rebated at 50 per cent.

B. If the stock price falls enough to cover transactions costs, the Put is exercised and the writer immediately sells the "Put" stock. The long position is closed out prior to end of the six-month holding period. Net profit (or loss) is taxed (rebated) at 50 per cent.

11. Sell Call

A. If the stock price does not rise enough to cover the option buyer's transactions costs, the option expires unexercised and the premium is ordinary income, taxed at 50 per cent.

B. If the stock price rises sufficiently, the option is exercised. The writer must buy stock in open market. Profit or loss is short-term and taxed (rebated) at 50 per cent.

12. Sell Put

A. If the stock price rises, remains unchanged, or does not fall sufficiently to cover the buyer's transactions costs, the option expires unexercised and the premium is ordinary income, taxed at 50 per cent.

B. If the stock price falls sufficiently, the option is exercised. The cost basis of stock is the striking price less premium. The writer then sells the "Put" stock at current market price. Net profit (or loss) is short-term and taxed (rebated) at 50 per cent.

Table 2-3 (Cont.)

---

13. Sell Straddle, Buy Stock
A. If both sides of the Straddle remain unexercised, the option premium is a short-term capital gain. The loss on long position (from transactions costs) is established as a short-term capital loss. Net profit is taxed at 50 per cent.
B. If the stock price rises enough so that the Call option is exercised, the profit from the expired Put option is a short-term capital gain and taxed at 50 per cent. The writer elects either 9B(1) or 9B(2) for tax treatment of profit from the Call option.
C. If the stock price falls enough so that the Put option is exercised, the writer disposes of the "Put" stock, suffering a short-term capital loss. The long position is closed out prior to six months to establish a short-term capital loss. The premium from the expired Call option is treated as a short-term capital gain. Net profit or loss is taxed at 50 per cent.

14. Sell Straddle
A. If both sides of the Straddle remain unexercised the total premium is a short-term capital gain and is taxed at 50 per cent.
B. If the stock price rises sufficiently so that the Call option is exercised, the capital gain or loss from the simultaneous sale of stock (at the striking price plus the Call premium) and purchase of stock at the market price is short-term. The premium from the Put side of the Straddle is a short-term capital gain. Total profit (or loss) is taxed (rebated) at 50 per cent.
C. If the stock price falls sufficiently so that the Put option is exercised, the capital gain or loss from the simultaneous purchase of stock at the striking price (minus the Put premium) and sale of stock at the market price is short-term. The premium from the Call option is short-term capital gain. Total profit (or loss) is taxed (rebated) at 50 per cent.

15. Buy Stock, Buy Put[1]
A. If the stock price rises, remains unchanged, or does not fall enough to cover transactions costs, the Put remains unexercised and its premium is added to the cost basis of the stock. If a net gain is realized, the stock will be sold after six months for a long-term capital gain and taxed at 25 per cent. If a net loss is realized, the stock will be sold prior to the end of the six-months holding period for a short-term capital loss, rebated at 50 per cent.
B. If the stock price falls sufficiently, the Put is exercised through the delivery of the shares originally acquired, prior to the end of the six-months holding period. Short-term capital loss is rebated at 50 per cent.

16. Sell Short, Buy Call
A. If the stock price rises sufficiently to make exercise of the Call profitable, the investor chooses the more favorable of the following alternatives:

71

Table 2-3 (Cont.)

---

16. (Cont.)
   1. The Call is exercised and stock is obtained to cover short position. The net loss is short-term and is rebated at 50 per cent.
   2. The Call is sold to a third party after six months for a long-term capital gain. The short sale is covered through the purchase of stock and a short-term capital loss is realized.
B. If the stock price falls, remains unchanged, or does not rise enough to make exercise of the Call profitable, the Call option is sold to a third party prior to the end of the six-month holding period for a short-term loss. The short sale is covered for a short-term capital gain (or loss). Net profits (or losses) are short-term and taxed (rebated) at 50 per cent.

---

[1] See Paragraph 653, U.S. Master Tax Guide, p. 312. It is assumed that both transactions are made simultaneously and the stock "identified" used if the Put is exercised.

CHAPTER THREE

Utility Functions, Decision Criteria, and Specification of the States of Nature

The previous chapter described the sixteen basic strategies that a hypothetical investor may employ and the calculation of the cash payoffs that accrue to him for each of his strategies and each stock price prevailing in the market six months and ten days after he has chosen a strategy. Clearly, what is optimal from an investor's point of view depends not only on the cash payoffs accruing to him but also on the utility he derives from the payoffs and on the decision criterion he employs for solving the game against nature.

The satisfaction that the individual derives from alternative gains and losses is summarized in his utility function. It is clear that an individual who obtains great satisfaction from large gains and does not experience great dissatisfaction from moderate losses will tend to behave differently than an individual upon whom moderate losses inflict great pain and who gets only moderate satisfaction from large gains.

When the individual is confronted with a whole array of possible outcomes (in utility terms), he must weight the consequences of his choices in terms of how "nature" may respond to him. Some may be pessimists and believe that, whatever they do, nature will punish them by producing the most unfavorable result consistent with their choice. Others may be optimistic and believe in the opposite outcome. The decision made by the individual will rest on some decision criterion that implicitly incorporates beliefs of this kind.

Consequently, in order to solve this game in which the investor picks investment strategies and "nature" picks stock prices, some assumptions must be made about utility functions and decision criteria. Moreover, it is necessary to specify the entire set of nature's strategies that may occur. These assumptions and some of their consequences are discussed in this chapter. In the final section, the description of the experiments to be performed is recapitulated.

3.1
Utility Functions

Since the outcome of the experiments depends crucially on the numerical magnitudes of the payoffs, it was not sufficient to specify some general properties that our utility functions have to obey. We had to select some specific functions. Considerations of economy compelled us to limit severely the number of different functions employed in the experiments. Nevertheless, experimentation was conducted with several types of utility functions, reflecting alternative individual attitudes.

The general properties built into our concrete utility functions concern the marginal utility of cash and its rate of change as cash payoffs increase. If we denote cash payoffs by x and the individual's utility function by $U(x)$, we shall assume throughout that the marginal utility of cash is positive:

$$U'(x) > 0.$$

In addition, an individual may have constant, increasing, or decreasing marginal utility of cash payoffs. Accordingly, we employ some utility functions with $U''(x) = 0$, some with $U''(x) > 0$, and some with $U''(x) < 0$, to reflect the various possibilities with respect to a change in marginal utility.

The general shape of the utility function as characterized by its first and second derivatives is also of relevance in the context in which we can define probabilities for the occurrence of the events that give the investor utility. The three cases characterized by $U''(x) = 0$, $U''(x) > 0$, and $U''(x) < 0$ correspond to the attitudes of risk neutrality, risk love, and risk aversion, respectively. This is so because, for example, an individual with a concave utility function

$(U''(x) < 0)$ would always prefer a sure outcome to a gamble which has the same actuarial value.

Various authors have made special assumptions about the curvature of the utility function in order to explain certain observable regularities such as the fact that the same person may insure against a risk with a low probability of a high loss and at the same time gamble on a risk with a low probability of a high gain. Relatively complicated shapes have been proposed by Friedman and Savage, Markowitz, and Rosett.[1] On the whole we shall investigate only simple types of utility functions, concentrating most of our effort on utility functions that are everywhere concave or convex and giving some attention to formulations with cubic shapes, that is, possessing a point of inflection.

Since, as indicated before, we need specific utility functions for numerical solutions of our games against nature, we selected some particular functions embodying the above assumptions about first and second partial derivatives. In addition we selected these functions so as to satisfy the normalization $U(0) = 0$ and $U(1) = 1$. This assumption was convenient because most of the positive cash payoffs are between 0 and 1. The normalization then assures that the resulting utility payoffs are of comparable magnitude, thus allowing results to reflect primarily differences in curvature.

The three basic types of utility functions chosen for experimentation were:

$$U(x) = x \tag{3.1}$$

$$U(x) = \frac{1 - e^{-ax} + x}{2 - e^{-a}} \tag{3.2}$$

$$U(x) = \frac{x + e^{ax} - 1}{e^a} \tag{3.3}$$

where a is a parameter, variations in which change the curvature of

---

[1] Milton Friedman and Leonard J. Savage, "The Utility Analysis of Choices Involving Risk," *J. of Political Economy* (August 1948) pp. 279–304; Harry Markowitz, "The Utility of Wealth," *J. of Political Economy* (April 1952) pp. 151–158; Richard N. Rosett, "Estimating the Utility of Wealth from Call Option Transactions," in Donald Hester and James Tobin, *Risk Aversion and Portfolio Choice* (New York: Wiley, 1967), pp. 154–169.

the utility function. We can verify immediately that the three types possess the required properties. From (3.1) we have $U'(x) = 1$ and $U''(x) = 0$. From (3.2) we have

$$U'(x) = \frac{1 + ae^{-ax}}{2 - e^{-a}}$$

which is positive for $a > 0$. Furthermore,

$$U''(x) = \frac{-a^2 e^{-ax}}{2 - e^{-a}} < 0$$

and (3.2) thus yields diminishing marginal utility. Finally, from (3.3) we have

$$U'(x) = \frac{1 + ae^{ax}}{e^a}$$

which is positive for $a > 0$ and

$$U''(x) = \frac{a^2 e^{ax}}{e^a} > 0$$

thus yielding increasing marginal utility. For the sake of simplicity, the three utility functions given by (3.1), (3.2), and (3.3) will be referred to as the CMU (constant marginal utility), DMU (diminishing marginal utility), and IMU (increasing marginal utility) utility functions respectively.

Some additional properties of (3.2) and (3.3) are worth noticing. Pratt[2] has introduced the function

$$r(x) = -\frac{U''(x)}{U'(x)}$$

which is a measure of local risk aversion. It has been argued that it is reasonable to believe that the premium an individual is willing to pay to insure against a given risk diminishes with the size of his assets. It has been shown that if this is true, his utility function must exhibit diminishing risk aversion. For (3.1) the function $r(x) = 0$. For (3.2) we have

$$r(x) = \frac{a^2 e^{-ax}}{1 + ae^{-ax}}$$

and

---

[2] John W. Pratt, "Risk Aversion in the Small and in the Large," *Econometrica* (January-April 1964) pp. 122–136.

$$r'(x) = \frac{-a^3 e^{-ax}}{(1 + ae^{-ax})^2} < 0 \qquad (3.4)$$

For (3.3) we obtain

$$r(x) = -\frac{a^2 e^{ax}}{1 + ae^{ax}}$$

and

$$r'(x) = \frac{-a^3 e^{ax}}{(1 + ae^{ax})^2} < 0 \qquad (3.5)$$

Clearly both (3.2) and (3.3) satisfy the condition of decreasing risk aversion. In the case of (3.2) the individual is risk averse and thus the meaning of (3.4) is the usual one. In the case of (3.3) the individual is not risk averse; that is, the premium he is willing to pay to insure against a risk is actually negative. This implies that as his assets increase he will require larger and larger compensation in order to stay away from taking a given risk: he has increasing risk love. It may be noted that we have not employed a quadratic utility function because, in spite of its otherwise desirable properties, it does not satisfy the condition of decreasing risk aversion.[3]

Both Rosett and Klevorick[4] have argued for the use of cubic utility functions. Thus, three additional utility functions were employed, each of them exhibiting generally "cubic" shape. The three functions are

$$U(x) = x^3 \qquad (3.6)$$

$$U(x) = \begin{cases} \dfrac{1 - e^{-ax} + x}{2 - e^{-a}} & \text{if } x \geqq 0 \\[3mm] -\dfrac{1 - e^{-a|x|} + |x|}{2 - e^{-a}} & \text{if } x < 0 \end{cases} \qquad (3.7)$$

$$U(x) = \begin{cases} \dfrac{x + e^{ax} - 1}{e^a} & \text{if } x \geqq 0 \\[3mm] -\dfrac{|x| + e^{a|x|} - 1}{e^a} & \text{if } x < 0 \end{cases} \qquad (3.8)$$

---

[3] *Ibid.*, p. 132.

[4] Rosett, "Estimating the Utility of Wealth" and Alvin K. Klevorick, "Capital Budgeting Under Risk: A Mathematical-Programming Approach," Econometric Research Program, Research Memorandum No. 89, Princeton University, September 1967, pp. 250–274.

Equations (3.6) and (3.8) exhibit risk love for gains and risk aversion for losses whereas (3.7) is of the opposite type, describing a person who is conservative (risk averse) with respect to gains and a gambler with respect to losses. The various properties of (3.7) and (3.8) can be obtained immediately from those of (3.2) and (3.3). It may also be verified that (3.6) is perverse in the sense that it exhibits increasing risk aversion. The utility function given by (3.6) will be referred to as the cubic utility function. Function (3.7), since it is composed of reflections of the DMU utility function, will be called the Composite DMU utility function. For analogous reasons, (3.8) will be referred to as the Composite IMU utility function.

Table 3-1

Utility Transformations for Selected Cash Payoffs
$(a = 1.6)$

Cash Payoffs and CMU Utility Function	DMU Utility Function	IMU Utility Function	CUBIC Utility Function	COMPOSITE DMU Utility Function	COMPOSITE IMU Utility Function
		Utility Values			
−2.500	−31.199	−0.703	−15.625	−1.936	−11.326
−2.000	−14.200	−0.597	−8.000	−1.646	−5.155
−1.500	−6.409	−0.486	−3.375	−1.340	−2.326
−1.000	−2.755	−0.363	−1.000	−1.000	−1.000
−0.500	−0.960	−0.212	−0.125	−0.584	−0.348
0.000	0.000	0.000	0.000	0.000	0.000
0.500	0.584	0.348	0.125	0.584	0.348
1.000	1.000	1.000	1.000	1.000	1.000
1.500	1.340	2.326	3.375	1.340	2.326
2.000	1.646	5.155	8.000	1.646	5.155
2.500	1.936	11.326	15.625	1.936	11.326

The actual utility functions employed in the various experiments are (3.1), (3.2), (3.3), (3.6), (3.7), and (3.8). For those that depend on a parameter a we alternately used the values 1.6 and 2.3.[5]

---

[5] It is shown in the Appendix that the higher the value of a the more "humped" or curved the utility function is in that range of payoff values in which most actual payoffs occur.

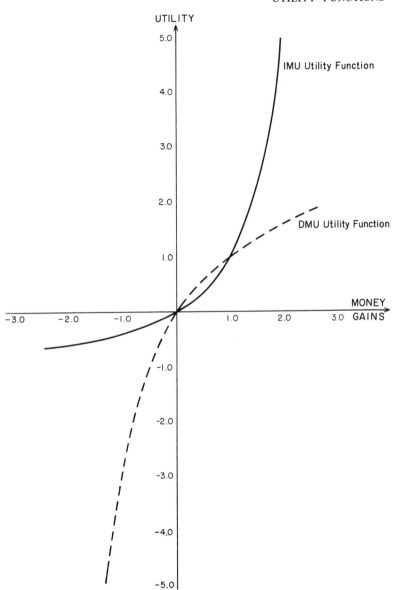

Figure 3-1
A comparison of the IMU *and* DMU *utility functions.*

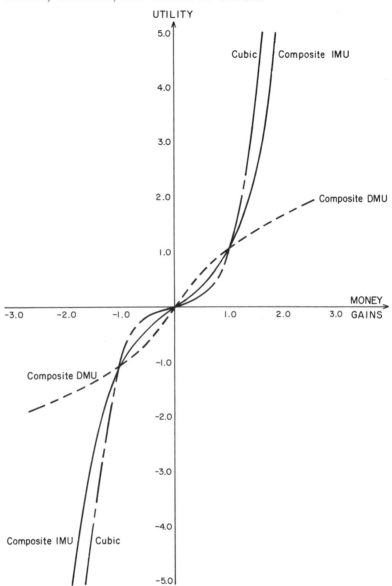

Figure 3-2

A comparison of the cubic, Composite IMU *and Composite* DMU *utility functions.*

Thus a total of ten different functions were employed. For each experiment, the cash payoffs were transformed into utility payoffs by employing alternately each of the ten utility functions.

Table 3-1 illustrates the transformations of cash payoffs into utility payoffs for the six main types of utility functions employed. The value of a in these transformations was 1.6. Figures 3-1 and 3-2 present these data visually.

It must be noted, however, that the fact that these utility functions exhibit, in turn, the general properties which we associate with the various kinds of attitudes toward risk does not suggest that the solutions derived by using these utility functions are in some sense "valid" for all persons with that particular attitude toward risk. Our experiments are more in the nature of an exhibition of broad conclusions with respect to the rationality of certain investment strategies.

3.2
Enumeration of the Possible States of Nature

In each experiment the individual investor can choose among the sixteen strategies that were discussed in Chapter 2. Nature's strategies consist of picking a market price for the security at the end of the 190-day holding period. Before we can proceed, it will be necessary to specify exactly how the set of possible nature's strategies is to be determined.

The first assumption we make is that nature produces only integral values for the stock price. This assumption, which makes it impossible for the closing price after 190 days to be a price such as $45\frac{5}{8}$, undoubtedly introduces some degree of coarseness into our analysis but allows us to limit nature's strategies to a manageable number.

In all the figures in Chapter 2 it was assumed that the pertinent range of nature's states was bounded by 10 points on either side of the striking price of the option. We call this the "0 Strategy Set" or more briefly the "0 Set" because the eleventh (middle) strategy of nature represents a zero price change. A range of plus or minus 10 points was chosen on the basis of an empirical investigation of actual 190-day price changes (from the start of the year) of all stocks on the New York Stock Exchange selling between $45 and $55 at the start of the period during years 1960 through 1964. It was found that 94 per cent of the actual price changes were contained within this range during those years when the general market level was relatively constant over the first six months and ten days. Nevertheless, it seemed desirable to investigate the effect of alternative values for the middle strategy of nature. Thus we also considered what we call the "+6 Strategy Set" and the "−6 Strategy Set." Here the total range of possible prices is from plus to minus 10 points from a middle value, which, however, is a price six points higher (lower) than the assumed striking price of $50. Consequently, in this case the investor is assumed to believe that the relevant states of nature

Table 3-2

Payoff Values for the Sixteen Strategies,
Per Dollar Invested
(cash-to-cash case; tax-exempt investor; no dividends; standard premium)

Strategy	1	2	3	4	5	6	7	8
Market Price of Common at End of Option Period	Cash	Buy Stock	Sell Stock (Short)	Buy Stock on Margin	Sell Stock (Short) on Margin	Buy Call	Buy Put	Buy Straddle
20	0.02	−0.61	0.59	−0.88	0.83	−1.00	5.50	1.82
35	0.02	−0.31	0.29	−0.46	0.40	−1.00	2.14	0.36
38	0.02	−0.26	0.22	−0.38	0.31	−1.00	1.47	0.07
41	0.02	−0.20	0.16	−0.29	0.22	−1.00	0.80	−0.22
44	0.02	−0.14	0.10	−0.21	0.14	−1.00	0.13	−0.51
47	0.02	−0.08	0.04	−0.12	0.05	−1.00	−0.54	−0.80
50	0.02	−0.02	−0.02	−0.04	−0.04	−1.00	−1.00	−1.00
53	0.02	0.04	−0.08	0.05	−0.13	−0.65	−1.00	−0.80
56	0.02	0.10	−0.14	0.13	−0.21	−0.14	−1.00	−0.51
59	0.02	0.16	−0.20	0.22	−0.30	0.37	−1.00	−0.22
62	0.02	0.22	−0.26	0.30	−0.39	0.88	−1.00	0.06
65	0.02	0.28	−0.32	0.39	−0.47	1.39	−1.00	0.35
80	0.02	0.58	−0.63	0.81	−0.91	3.94	−1.00	1.80

leave him more to gain than to fear (in that more of nature's states are above the striking price than below). He is still assumed to be ignorant of the probabilities with which each of nature's states occurs. In an empirical analysis of actual price changes over the first six months of the year(s) between 1960 and 1964 when the market advanced (declined) it was found that the $+6$ Strategy Set (-6 Strategy Set) range encompassed approximately 95 per cent of the actual price changes. In Table 3-2 the payoff values for the 16 strategies are shown for a wide range of alternative market prices.

It also seemed desirable to treat a case where the range of possible payoffs was wider than plus or minus 10 points from the center of the distribution. We arbitrarily chose a range of plus or

Table 3-2 (continued)

Strategy	9	10	11	12	13	14	15	16
Market Price of Common at End of Option Period	Sell Call Buy Stock	Sell Put Buy Stock	Sell Call	Sell Put	Sell Strad-dle Buy Stock	Sell Strad-dle	Buy Stock Buy Put	Sell Stock Buy Call
20	−0.56	−1.24	0.54	−3.12	−1.27	−3.68	−0.10	0.42
35	−0.23	−0.60	0.54	−1.39	−0.55	−1.15	−0.10	0.15
38	−0.17	−0.47	0.54	−1.04	−0.40	−0.64	−0.10	0.09
41	−0.10	−0.34	0.54	−0.70	−0.26	−0.13	−0.10	0.04
44	−0.04	−0.21	0.54	−0.35	−0.11	0.38	−0.10	−0.01
47	0.03	−0.09	0.54	−0.01	0.03	0.89	−0.10	−0.07
50	0.10	0.06	0.54	0.45	0.20	1.55	−0.10	−0.12
53	0.10	0.13	0.13	0.45	0.20	0.88	−0.04	−0.12
56	0.10	0.19	−0.17	0.45	0.20	0.37	0.01	−0.12
59	0.10	0.26	−0.48	0.45	0.20	−0.14	0.06	−0.12
62	0.10	0.32	−0.79	0.45	0.20	−0.65	0.12	−0.12
65	0.10	0.38	−1.10	0.45	0.20	−1.16	0.17	−0.12
80	0.10	0.71	−2.64	0.45	0.20	−3.72	0.45	−0.12

minus 30 points from the striking price and call this the "extended-range" case. This range included practically all the realized outcomes during the first halves of years 1960 through 1964. This kind of case was treated in order to examine whether the optimal strategies are significantly influenced by changes in the range of nature's strategies. In this extended-range case nature's strategy set is assumed to be even coarser than in the standard-range case; the unit of price differences is now three dollars. A problem emerging from the extended-range case is that, if investors actually believed that a particular stock was likely to be very much more volatile than a standard $50 stock, the option premiums that were used to do the calculations would undoubtedly not apply. This is so because, if the characteristic price volatility for a security was extraordinarily large, the relevant option premiums would undoubtedly be higher than those used in our examples. Indeed, the cross-section analysis of option premiums, reported in Section 1.6, indicated that premiums tend to increase with the past volatility of the underlying common stock. To determine the effect of this dependence of the premium on the range of the states of nature considered possible, we performed two types of experiments for the extended-range case: First, we hypothesized that the range of nature's states was extended but we employed the standard option premium to calculate the payoffs. Then we repeated the experiment with a larger option premium. The increase in the option premium was determined by the volatility coefficients estimated in the cross-sectional study described in Section 1.6. The increase in volatility implied by the change from the "standard" to the "extended" range was multiplied by the estimated volatility coefficient to find the increase in the option premium that would be likely to accompany the hypothesized increase in the expected range of price fluctuations.

It might be thought that defining nature's strategies as we have done already implies a prior distribution over future stock prices, thus contradicting the assumption that the investor has no such prior distribution. But, clearly, in any game against nature one must define what nature's strategies are and, by implication, what they are not. These definitions may assign zero probability to some (potential) outcomes. To this extent then all games against nature involve some minimal prior information.

3.3
Decision Criteria

The various methods that can be used to solve games against nature are discussed fully in several works,[6] and it will suffice to give a brief statement of each method. Each solution method arises from one of the decision criteria that are outlined below. In the discussion that follows a_{ij} denotes the payoff (in utility terms) to the investor if he employs his ith and nature its jth pure strategy. We assume that the investor has m and nature n possible pure strategies.

1. The minimax criterion. According to this criterion the individual seeks a probability vector or mixed strategy $p = (p_1, \ldots, p_m)$, such that, irrespective of the price chosen by nature, the expected value of the game, $\sum_{i=1}^{m} p_i a_{ij}$, for him is not less than a quantity V

$$\sum_{i=1}^{m} p_i a_{ij} \geqq V \quad \text{for } j = 1, \ldots, n$$

and that, of all such vectors p, the quantity V is as large as possible. In the special case in which there exists a pair of indices i' and j' such that $a_{i'j'} = \max_i \min_j a_{ij} = \min_j \max_i a_{ij}$, the solution for the probability vector p will contain one element equal to unity and the rest equal to zero, thus yielding a pure strategy.

2. The minimax regret criterion applies the minimax criterion to a matrix derived from the matrix $\|a_{ij}\|$ on the basis of the assumption that what matters to the individual are not the utility payoffs but rather the "regrets" he experiences. Regret is defined as the deprivation of utility the decision-maker experiences by making some strategic choice rather than the best choice he could have made if he had known what strategy nature would select. Thus each element a_{ij} will be replaced by $a_{ij} - \max_k a_{kj}$.

3. The Hurwicz criterion requires the individual to qualify the degree of his optimism by specifying a coefficient α, $0 \leqq \alpha \leqq 1$, where $\alpha = 1$ represents complete optimism and $\alpha = 0$ complete pessimism.

---

[6] John Milnor, "Games Against Nature," in *Decision Processes*, ed. by R. M. Thrall, C. H. Coombs and R. L. Davis (New York: Wiley, 1954) pp. 49–59; R. Duncan Luce and Howard Raiffa, *Games and Decisions* (New York: Wiley, 1957) pp. 275–326.

According to this criterion, he weights the best and worst payoff for each of his pure strategies by α and $1 - \alpha$ respectively, i.e., computes for each i the quantity $\alpha \max_j a_{ij} + (1 - \alpha)\min_j a_{ij}$ and chooses that one of his pure strategies for which this quantity is largest. Three values of α were employed: 0.75, 0.50, and 0.25.

4. According to the Laplace criterion the individual maximizes expected utility on the assumption that all of nature's strategies are equally likely. Thus the individual will choose his kth pure strategy if $\sum_{j=1}^{n} a_{kj} > \sum_{j=1}^{n} a_{ij}$ for all $i \neq k$.

5. As a final decision criterion, we assumed that the decision-maker may employ some particular prior distribution, other than the uninformative prior, over the strategies of nature and choose on the basis of maximum expected utility. We utilized a distribution of nature's strategies that was derived from observing the relative frequency of stock price changes over a 190-day period of all securities which sold at a price between $45 and $55 on the New York Stock Exchange on the first trading day of the years 1960 through 1964. The relative frequencies employed are shown in Table 3-3. As another alternative we employed several other distributions derived from the normal distribution and differing from each other in terms of the value of the standard deviation.

The computation of solutions by the various decision criteria is straightforward. The minimax and minimax regret solutions can be obtained by formulating a suitable linear programming[7] problem and the other solutions by even simpler arithmetic operations. A much more serious difficulty is that there is no empirical evidence concerning what decision criteria individuals might employ in practice. Even more serious is the difficulty that no obvious choice among the criteria is possible even from the purely normative point of view. Thus each of the criteria violates some reasonable condition that we might wish to consider an axiom of human behavior.

The meaning and reasonableness of the axioms has been

---

[7] The solution of the dual problem provides us with the "optimal strategies" of nature. Since it is difficult to think of the investor's and nature's positions as fully symmetric, no attempt was made to interpret the dual solution in the context of reality.

Table 3-3

**Relative Frequencies of 190-Day Price Changes
for All Stocks Selling Between $45 and $55**
As of January 1 of Each Year, 1960–1964

Price Change[1]	Relative Frequency
−30	0.003
−27	0.003
−24	0.005
−21	0.017
−18	0.017
−15	0.036
−12	0.043
−9	0.053
−6	0.072
−3	0.101
0	0.111
+3	0.152
+6	0.157
+9	0.087
+12	0.075
+15	0.048
+18	0.007
+21	0.005
+24	0.001
+27	0.002
+30	0.005

[1] Each class interval includes all price changes within 1½ points of the amount indicated in the column.

discussed clearly by Luce and Raiffa,[8] and we have little to add to this discussion. It will be sufficient to remind the reader of what particular axioms the various criteria violate. First, the minimax regret criterion, which we also find intuitively the least appealing, violates the axiom of the Independence of Irrelevant Alternatives. That is to say, if a decision problem were to be redefined by simply adding a new pure strategy to the individual's already existing repertoire of pure strategies, we might find that a formerly nonoptimal strategy becomes optimal. The Laplace criterion violates the axiom

[8] Luce and Raiffa, *Games and Decisions*, pp. 286–298.

of Column Duplication and thus produces solutions which are not invariant with respect to duplicate or multiple occurrences of some pure strategy of nature's. This kind of difficulty may be the result of incorrect enumeration of nature's possible strategies. Fortunately, in the present context this is hardly likely, since nature's pure strategies are defined in terms of discrete price levels, no two of which can produce the same set of payoffs. Finally, the minimax criterion and the Hurwicz criterion violate the axiom of Column Linearity. This axiom states that the individual's optimal strategy should not change as a result of adding a constant to some particular column of the payoff matrix, that is, to the (utility) payoffs of some particular pure strategy of nature. Although this axiom appears intuitively far less obviously desirable than some of the others, it can be shown that it is equivalent to the following requirement: that the optimal strategy of the individual in a given game against nature be the same as that in a new game which consists of a chance combination of either having to play the given game or another game the payoffs of which are such that no action by the individual makes any difference for him.[9]

We cannot argue convincingly that one axiom is ultimately more reasonable than another. In the final analysis this is a somewhat personal matter. The general reasonableness of all the relevant axioms has been argued convincingly by Luce and Raiffa. Although we may feel that Column Linearity is perhaps somewhat less compelling than the Independence of Irrelevant Alternatives, we cannot rest basic procedural decisions in our experiments on such an infirm basis. For this reason, every one of the games was solved by employing, in turn, each of the decision criteria. This choice is unavoidable in the light of (1) absence of empirical evidence as to how the preponderance of individuals would make decisions in games against nature and (2) our inability to go further in a purely theoretical-normative sense in choosing among alternative criteria.

---

[9] *Ibid.*, pp. 290–292.

3.4
Are Utility Functions and Decision Criteria Mutually Independent?

A final difficulty remains to be settled. The shape of the utility function is often interpreted in casual terms as representing "conservative" or "unconservative" attitudes. In this casual sense a person who prefers a small but sure gain to potentially large but uncertain gains may thus be called financially conservative. Risk aversion, as indicated by a negative sign for $U''(x)$, is termed conservative behavior because the individual with such a utility function rejects a gamble with a certain expected value in favor of a sure thing with the same (expected) value.

At the same time, the choice of the minimax criterion is thought to reflect a pessimistic view of nature. Indeed, the minimax criterion has been criticized for implying "conservative" behavior. It may be asked, then, whether we are justified in experimenting with all possible combinations of utility functions and decision criteria: are not some of them inconsistent with each other? Specifically, may one assume, even in some hypothetical experiment, that an unconservative individual with a convex (IMU) utility function (that is, a risk lover) employs the minimax criterion? The position taken here is that the utility function and the decision criterion are independent. The former assigns utility or a satisfaction level to events and is independent of the subjective (or objective) probabilities associated with events. The latter reflects the individual's views concerning the ease or difficulty of realizing various events. There is thus no inconsistency in assuming that the individual is "conservative" with respect to the decision criterion he employs and "unconservative" with respect to his utility function. Nevertheless, as we shall indicate in Section 4.4.4, certain utility functions may lead the investor to choose the same types of strategies that may be implied by particular decision criteria.

3.5
A Recapitulation of the Experiments
To Be Performed

Before turning to an analysis of our results, it will be useful to recapitulate the different types of experiments to be performed. As noted, the general approach of this study will be to perform computer experiments which simulate a variety of market conditions and different states of expectations, employ various criteria of investor rationality under uncertainty, and hypothesize various kinds of utility functions on the part of investors. We shall then determine which investment strategy is optimal under the conditions postulated. In this way we shall try to ascertain the proper role of stock options in an investor's portfolio.

The experiments differ with respect to the following specific assumptions:

1. *Utility function of decision-maker.* Six alternative types of utility functions are employed. Either we assume utility to be linear in money or we assume that there is increasing or decreasing marginal utility of dollar payoffs. In addition, we employ a cubic utility function and two types of composite functions. The degree to which the utility function exhibits increasing or decreasing marginal utility of money is controlled by varying a parameter of the function.

2. *Decision criterion employed by the individual investor.* Assuming that the decision problem is a true game against nature, we shall alternatively employ the Laplace, minimax, minimax regret, and Hurwicz criteria. In addition, we treated the situation as one of risk rather than uncertainty. The optimal strategy for an investor will be taken to be that which offers the highest expected utility for selected prior distributions and for a calculated a posteriori probability distribution.

3. *Enumeration of the set of nature's states.* Four alternative sets of "strategies" for nature were employed. The "0 Strategy Set" assumed that the possible range of nature's states is bounded by 10 points on either side of the striking price of the option. In the +6 and −6 cases the central strategy of nature is a price six points higher or lower than the striking price of the option. In the extended-range

case possible future stock prices may be as much as 30 points above and below the striking price of the option. In experiments where the extended range was employed, payoffs were calculated on the basis of both the standard (average) option premium and a larger premium consistent with the greater characteristic volatility of the underlying common.

4. *Initial and final position of the investor.* In the "cash-to-cash" experiment the investor is assumed to begin the investment period with a portfolio consisting entirely of cash and to close out any long or short position at the end of the six-month ten-day holding period, so that he ends up with a portfolio again consisting entirely of cash. In the "stock-to-stock" case the investor's initial and final positions will be assumed to be a round lot of common stock.

5. *Tax bracket of the investor.* Two different assumptions are used. In the tax-exempt case the investor is assumed to pay no taxes on his gains and to receive no tax rebate on losses. In the taxable case the investor is assumed to be in a 50 per cent marginal tax bracket and to have already taken sufficient capital gains so that he may deduct all losses from realized gains.

6. *Dividend payment on the common stock.* Experiments are performed under the alternative assumptions that the common pays either no dividend or dividends at a rate equal to the average dividend yield of the Standard & Poor industrial average.

Appendix

Utility functions (3.2) and (3.3) both depend upon a parameter a. Variations in this parameter alter the shape of the utility function in a systematic way. Both functions become more "humped" in the region $0 < x < 1$ as a increases. Function (3.2) becomes steeper to the left of the origin and flatter for $x > 1$, whereas the converse is true for (3.3).

In order to prove these assertions it is sufficient to examine the rate of change of the function with respect to a. We treat separately the two principal utility functions.

Increasing Marginal Utility. Given

$$U = \frac{x + e^{ax} - 1}{e^a}$$

we differentiate and, rearranging, obtain

$$\frac{\partial U}{\partial a} = \frac{(e^{ax} - 1)(x - 1)}{e^a} \tag{3A.1}$$

Since $a > 0$, it follows that

$$\frac{\partial U}{\partial a} > 0 \quad \text{if } x > 1$$

$$\frac{\partial U}{\partial a} < 0 \quad \text{if } 0 < x < 1$$

$$\frac{\partial U}{\partial a} > 0 \quad \text{if } x < 0$$

as is required by our assertion.

Diminishing Marginal Utility. The relevant function in this case is

$$U = \frac{1 - e^{-ax} + x}{2 - e^{-a}}$$

Differentiating with respect to a we obtain

$$\frac{\partial U}{\partial a} = \frac{xe^{-ax}(2 - e^{-a}) - e^{-a}(1 + x - e^{-ax})}{(2 - e^{-a})^2} \tag{3A.2}$$

It is sufficient to examine the sign of the numerator. The numerator may be rewritten as

$$\phi = xe^{-ax}e^{-a}\left[(e^a - e^{ax}) + \left(e^a - 1 + \frac{1 - e^{ax}}{x}\right)\right] \tag{3A.3}$$

Thus the sign of ϕ is given by the sign of $x[A(x) + B(x)]$ where

$$A(x) = e^a - e^{ax}$$

and

$$B(x) = e^a - 1 + \frac{1 - e^{ax}}{x}$$

It is apparent that $A(x) + B(x)$ vanishes for $x = 1$. Since $a > 0$, it also follows that

$$A(x) > 0 \quad \text{if } x < 1$$
$$A(x) < 0 \quad \text{if } x > 1$$

Now let $C(x) = xB(x) = 1 - e^{ax} + xe^a - x$. The equation $C(x) = 0$ obviously has 0 and 1 as roots. Moreover, these are its only real roots since $C'(x) = -ae^{ax} + e^a - 1$, which is monotone decreasing in x. Clearly, $B(x)$ vanishes only for $x = 1$. Thus $B(x)$ does not change sign for any $x > 1$ and does not change sign for any $x < 1$. But, clearly, for sufficiently large value of x we have $B(x) < 0$. Moreover, $B(0) = e^a - 1 - a > 0$. Hence, summarizing,

$$A(x) + B(x) < 0 \quad \text{for } x > 1$$
$$A(x) + B(x) > 0 \quad \text{for } x < 1$$

Since $\phi = xe^{-ax}e^{-a}[A(x) + B(x)]$, it follows that

$$\phi < 0 \quad \text{for } x > 1$$
$$\phi > 0 \quad \text{for } 0 < x < 1$$
$$\phi < 0 \quad \text{for } x < 0$$

Since $\partial U/\partial a$ has the same sign as ϕ, the assertion is proved.

CHAPTER FOUR
Analysis of Basic Results

In the previous chapters we discussed the history and characteristics of the option market and formulated the details of our approach to the problem of rational decision-making in securities markets. This approach rests on the assumption that the individual investor plays a game against nature in which his acts are defined by the securities (or options on securities) that he purchases or sells and those of nature are defined by the market prices prevailing at the horizon. It remains for us to analyze the solutions to the many different games we solved and to suggest how these results might offer guidance to actual investors. The games that we solved may be classified, somewhat arbitrarily perhaps, into a group of basic games and a group dealing with various realistic extensions and modifications. The present chapter deals with the results of the former group of games.

4.1
Introduction

A particular game is defined by the combination of "circumstances" that is supposed to prevail for some individual investor. These circumstances include the initial and final positions of the investor (cash-to-cash or stock-to-stock), the absence or presence of dividends or taxes, the specific range of alternatives available to nature ($+6$, 0, -6, or extended-range Strategy Set for nature), the investor's utility function, and the decision criterion he employs. Results from games may usefully be discussed in at least three ways.

First, one may examine carefully the solution of a number of individual games, for it may be interesting to know what the optimal strategy is when, for example, the game is cash-to-cash, the $+6$ Strategy Set for nature is employed, the investor has a linear utility function and uses the minimax regret criterion. Second, one may find it revealing to average the solutions over a large number of games, representing a variety of circumstances. We would then attempt to offer interpretations of the "average solutions." Third, one may determine how the solution changes when one or more of the circumstances defining the game is altered. We would then, for example, ask what happens to the solution of the game as we change the utility function from one that is linear in money payoffs to one exhibiting increasing marginal utility of money, holding all other circumstances constant.

The first type of analysis, that is, examination of the results of individual games, would be the most interesting and relevant for a particular investor who actually planned to act in the market in accord with the decision criterion employed in some particular game. However, it is very difficult to generalize from the solution of a single game, just as there is practically no generalizable content of theoretical interest in the solution of a single linear programming problem arising in operations research. Moreover, the individual games we have solved are special because of certain simplifying assumptions, such as the assumption that the investor's income is taxed at a 50 per cent rate, that he has a specific type of utility function, and so forth. These special characteristics tend to reduce the normative significance of the solution of a single game.

For these reasons more interest attaches, perhaps, to interpretations of the second and third types, particularly since the change in the solution to be expected when some circumstance of the game is altered is in some cases independently predictable on more or less ad hoc grounds derived, possibly, from stock market lore. One may thus test the soundness of more or less intuitive arguments about optimal behavior, and it should be possible to develop rules for improving investment performance.

Some of these comparisons will be presented in this chapter and we shall attempt to explain the change in the optimal strategy or strategies that results from alteration of such factors as the decision-maker's utility function and tax status. But it is fairly clear that it is not practical to make all possible pairwise comparisons since the number of such comparisons would be enormous.[1] Thus we shall not compare the solutions to pairs of games that vary only with respect to a single characteristic or circumstance. Instead we shall divide the set or some appropriately defined subset of all games into two groups according to that characteristic the variation in which is of interest. Then, rather than holding all other characteristics constant, we shall aggregate the solutions over all other characteristics.

A simplified example will clarify the nature of this procedure. Suppose that there were only two utility functions U_1 and U_2 and three decision criteria D_1, D_2, and D_3. Let us further suppose that the number of acts (pure strategies) available to the investor were four. Thus, the optimal solution (mixed strategy) of a game can be stated as a four-element vector of probability weights to be assigned to the four pure strategies. Assume for the sake of illustration that the optimal solutions of the six possible games are as follows:

Games	Solution
U_1D_1	(.74, .24, .02, 0.0)
U_1D_2	(1.00, 0.0, 0.0, 0.0)
U_1D_3	(0.0, 0.0, 1.00, 0.0)
U_2D_1	(.12, .18, .70, 0.0)
U_2D_2	(0.0, .20, .80, 0.0)
U_2D_3	(0.0, 1.00, 0.0, 0.0)

To compare the effect of substituting the utility function U_2 for the utility function U_1 we compute the *average optimal strategy* for U_1, that is, we average over the games U_1D_1, U_1D_2, U_1D_3 and similarly for U_2, yielding

Games	Average Solution
$U_1D_{1,2,3}$	(.58, .08, .34, 0.0)
$U_2D_{1,2,3}$	(.04, .46, .50, 0.0)

Here the quantity .58, which is the first element in the first average

---

[1] If we restrict ourselves to the standard range, cash-to-cash, tax-exempt case alone, we have 180 games (3 alternative sets of nature's strategies, 10 utility functions, 6 decision criteria) yielding $180 \times 179/2 = 16,110$ pairwise comparisons.

solution vector, is simply the unweighted arithmetic mean of the first elements in the three U_1 solution vectors; i.e., $.58 = (.74 + 1.00 + 0.0)/3.0$. Similarly, if we were interested in the effect of variation in the decision criterion, we would, separately for D_1, D_2, and D_3, average solutions over U_1 and U_2, yielding

Games	Average Solution
$U_{1,2}D_1$	(.43, .21, .36, 0.0)
$U_{1,2}D_2$	(.50, .10, .40, 0.0)
$U_{1,2}D_3$	(0.0, .50, .50, 0.0)

These average solutions have no normative significance, but they do represent the average behavior that would be observed among many investors if the various "other characteristics" over which we aggregate occurred in the population with equal frequency. These averages may thus be taken to be crude representations of average behavior in a population the characteristics of which (with respect to utility functions, decision criteria, etc.) we do not know, but concerning which we believe that a variety of more or less plausible circumstances are equally likely to occur. We are, in effect, acting as Bayesians with an uninformative prior distribution over the types of games that one is likely to encounter. Since our actual games employed 16 investor's strategies, many of our conclusions will rest on comparisons of two 16-component vectors which are averages over several games.

The specific comparisons we shall make in the present chapter are the following: (1) The cash-to-cash case with the stock-to-stock case, with no taxes or dividends in either; (2) the tax-exempt stock-to-stock case with the taxable stock-to-stock case, with no dividends in either; (3) the taxable stock-to-stock case with dividends with the same case without dividends; (4) the normal-range cash-to-cash case with the extended-range cash-to-cash case; (5) comparisons where the utility function is the variable characteristic; (6) comparisons where the decision criterion is the variable characteristic. In the next chapter we examine (7) the effect of changes in the expected variance of future stock prices; (8) the effect of differences in the size of the option premium; and (9) the effect of removing the prohibition against interim trading during the option period.

Table 4-1

Investor's Optimal Strategy Sets for Alternative
Utility Functions and Strategy Sets for Nature
(cash-to-cash case: tax-exempt investor)

A. Minimax and Minimax Regret Decision Criteria

Utility Function	Minimax +6 Strategy[2]	Proba-bility	Minimax 0 Strategy	Proba-bility	Minimax −6 Strategy	Proba-bility
1. IMU 2.3[1]	6 BC	.060	6 BC	.057	7 BP	.076
	12 SP	.610	7 BP	.031	11 SC	.521
	14 SSTR	.330	11 SC	.428	14 SSTR	.403
			12 SP	.483		
2. CMU	12 SP	.782	1 C	1.000	11 SC	.800
	14 SSTR	.218			14 SSTR	.200
3. DMU 2.3	1 C	1.000	1 C	1.000	11 SC	.781
					13 SSTR,BS	.219

Utility Function	Minimax Regret +6		Minimax Regret 0		Minimax Regret −6	
4. IMU 2.3	6 BC	.506	7 BP	.230	7 BP	.860
	14 SSTR	.494	14 SSTR	.770	14 SSTR	.140
5. CMU	6 BC	.002	1 C	.286	7 BP	.241
	12 SP	.998	11 SC	.429	11 SC	.759
			14 SSTR	.285		
6. DMU 2.3	12 SP	.423	1 C	.701	7 BP	.057
	13 SSTR,BS	.577	11 SC	.143	11 SC	.943
			14 SSTR	.156		

B. Laplace and Hurwicz Decision Criteria

Utility Function	Laplace +6	Laplace 0	Laplace −6	Hurwicz α = .25 +6	Hurwicz α = .25 0	Hurwicz α = .25 −6
7. IMU 2.3	6 BC	14 SSTR	7 BP	6 BC	14 SSTR	7 BP
8. CMU	12 SP	14 SSTR	11 SC	13 SSTR,BS	14 SSTR	11 SC
9. DMU 2.3	12 SP	14 SSTR	11 SC	13 SSTR,BS	1 C	11 SC

Utility Function	Hurwicz α = .50 +6	Hurwicz α = .50 0	Hurwicz α = .50 −6	Hurwicz α = .75 +6	Hurwicz α = .75 0	Hurwicz α = .75 −6
10. IMU 2.3	6 BC	14 SSTR	7 BP	6 BC	14 SSTR	7 BP
11. CMU	6 BC	14 SSTR	7 BP	6 BC	14 SSTR	7 BP
12. DMU 2.3	12 SP	14 SSTR	11 SC	12 SP	14 SSTR	11 SC

[1] The number 2.3 refers to the value of the parameter a in equations (3.2) and (3.3).

[2] For the meaning of the strategy numbers and abbreviations see Table 2-1, page 35.

4.2
Analysis of Individual Experiments

Tables 4-1, 4-2, and 4-3 present a sample of results from our computer experiments. The numbers in the tables represent the optimal strategies for a tax-exempt investor whose initial and final positions are in cash. In Table 4-1 we hold the decision criterion constant and vary the investor's attitude toward risk by reading down the columns or vary the center of the distribution of expected stock prices by reading along each row. The same results are presented in Table 4-2. Here the distributions are held constant and the reader may see the effect of variation in the decision criterion by reading down the columns and of variation in the investor's attitude toward risk by looking along the rows. In Table 4-3 we present the results for the extended-range case, where possible future stock prices may be as much as 30 points above and below the central price. In the appendix, Tables 4A-1 through 4A-3 present the same experiment for a taxable investor in the 50 per cent (marginal) tax bracket. Tables 4A-4 and 4A-5 present some sample results for the stock-to-stock case. Tables 4A-6 and 4A-7 present additional results for an investor with a Composite IMU utility function.

A fair degree of detail is presented in these tables so that the reader may begin to check his intuition against some results. Although, as was indicated in the previous section, we ascribe only modest importance to any single result, the totality of individual results is suggestive at least qualitatively.

We note, first of all, that the optimal strategies for the minimax and minimax regret criteria often involve mixed strategies. The natural interpretation of this phenomenon is the usual one, that the investor employs a suitable randomizing device for choosing among the possible pure strategies.[2] An alternative interpretation is that if many investors apply the minimax criterion independently of one

---

[2] For example, in the +6 Strategy Set with the minimax criterion and IMU utility function with $a = 2.3$ the investor would need a 3-digit random number. If the randomizing device produced a number between 000 and 059 inclusive, he would select Strategy 6; if the random number were between 060 and 669 he would choose Strategy 12 and otherwise he would select Strategy 14. If the investor employed such a randomizing device, he would select strategies on the average with the relative frequencies indicated in Table 4-1.

Table 4-2

Investor's Optimal Strategies for Alternative Decision Criteria and Utility Functions (cash-to-cash case: tax-exempt investor)

Decision Criterion	IMU 2.3[1]		CMU		DMU 2.3	
	Strategy	Probability	Strategy	Probability	Strategy	Probability
+6 Strategy Set						
Minimax	6 BC	.060	12 SP	.782	1 C	1.000
	12 SP	.610	14 SSTR	.218		
	14 SSTR	.330				
Minimax Regret	6 BC	.506	6 BC	.002	12 SP	.423
	14 SSTR	.494	12 SP	.998	13 SSTR,BS	.579
Hurwicz $\alpha = .25$	6 BC	1.000	13 SSTR,BS	1.000	13 SSTR,BS	1.000
Hurwicz $\alpha = .50$	6 BC	1.000	6 BC	1.000	12 SP	1.000
Hurwicz $\alpha = .75$	6 BC	1.000	6 BC	1.000	12 SP	1.000
Laplace	6 BC	1.000	12 SP	1.000	12 SP	1.000
0 Strategy Set						
Minimax	6 BC	.057	1 C	1.000	1 C	1.000
	7 BP	.031				
	11 SC	.429				
	12 SP	.483				
Minimax Regret	7 BP	.230	1 C	.286	1 C	.701
	14 SSTR	.770	11 SC	.429	11 SC	.143
			14 SSTR	.285	14 SSTR	.156

Hurwicz $\alpha = .25$	14 SSTR	1.000	14 SSTR	1.000	1 C	1.000
Hurwicz $\alpha = .50$	14 SSTR	1.000	14 SSTR	1.000	14 SSTR	1.000
Hurwicz $\alpha = .75$	14 SSTR	1.000	14 SSTR	1.000	14 SSTR	1.000
Laplace	14 SSTR	1.000	14 SSTR	1.000	14 SSTR	1.000
—6 Strategy Set						
Minimax	7 BP	.076	11 SC	.800	11 SC	.781
	11 SC	.521	14 SSTR	.200	13 SSTR,BS	.219
	14 SSTR	.403				
Minimax Regret	7 BP	.860	7 BP	.241	7 BP	.057
	14 SSTR	.140	11 SC	.759	11 SC	.943
Hurwicz $\alpha = .25$	7 BP	1.000	11 SC	1.000	11 SC	1.000
Hurwicz $\alpha = .50$	7 BP	1.000	7 BP	1.000	11 SC	1.000
Hurwicz $\alpha = .75$	7 BP	1.000	7 BP	1.000	11 SC	1.000
Laplace	7 BP	1.000	11 SC	1.000	11 SC	1.000

[1] The number 2.3 refers to the value of the parameter a in equations (3.2) and (3.3).

Table 4-3

Investor's Optimal Strategies for Extended-Range Strategy Set
(cash-to-cash case: tax-exempt investor)

Decision Criterion	Risk Level									
	IMU 2.3[1]		IMU 1.6[1]		CMU		DMU 1.6		DMU 2.3	
	Strategy	Probability	Strategy	Probability	Strategy	Probability	Strategy	Probability	Strategy	Probability
Minimax	6 BC	.033	6 BC	.065	7 BP	.345	5 SS	.232	1 C	1.000
	7 BP	.054	7 BP	.092	12 SP	.628	10 SP,BS	.051		
	11 SC	.394	11 SC	.368	14 SSTR	.027	16 SS,BC	.717		
	12 SP	.519	12 SP	.475						
Minimax Regret	7 BP	1.000	6 BC	.077	6 BC	.432	15 BS,BP	.321	15 BS,BP	.106
			7 BP	.923	7 BP	.568	16 SS,BC	.611	16 SS,BC	.735
							7 BP	.068	7 BP	.159
Hurwicz α = .25	7 BP	1.000	7 BP	1.000	7 BP	1.000	1 C	1.000	1 C	1.000
Hurwicz α = .50	7 BP	1.000	7 BP	1.000	7 BP	1.000	7 BP	1.000	15 BS,BP	1.000
Hurwicz α = .75	7 BP	1.000	7 BP	1.000	7 BP	1.000	7 BP	1.000	7 BP	1.000
Laplace	7 BP	1.000	7 BP	1.000	7 BP	1.000	15 BS,BP	1.000	15 BS,BP	1.000

[1]The numbers 2.3 and 1.6 refer to values of the parameter a in equations (3.2) and (3.3).

another, the probabilities representing the optimal strategy stand for the relative frequency with which the various strategies will be observed in reality. Thus, in the population of investors characterized by the +6 Strategy Set and the IMU utility function ($a = 2.3$) and who employ the minimax criterion, 6 per cent will buy a Call, 61 per cent will sell a Put, and 33 per cent will sell a Straddle (Table 4-1, Column 1). Indeed, if we knew the relative frequency of individuals and games with various characteristics, we could use this type of information to construct the demand and supply functions for the several types of options.

The most striking feature of the individual results displayed in Tables 4-1, 4-2, and 4-3 is the prevalence of solutions that involve the investor in dealing in options. In only four of the 54 different cases or games summarized in Table 4-1 is it true that neither the purchase nor the sale of options is optimal, either by itself or as part of a mixed strategy. A similar result holds for the extended-range case shown in Table 4-3 where option buying or selling is in the optimal strategy set in 27 out of 30 cases.

It is difficult to explain the differences between certain pairs of individual games. Thus from Table 4-2 we observe that for the 0 Strategy Set and the IMU utility function, the minimax criterion requires the investor to buy Calls, buy Puts, sell Calls, and sell Puts, whereas the minimax regret criterion has him buy Puts and sell Straddles. It is not clear intuitively why using the regret criterion makes Straddles more favorable than a combination of Puts and Calls, whereas the reverse is the case with the ordinary minimax criterion.

Examination of individual games makes it tempting to consider the meaning of the dual solution to the linear programming problems which have to be solved to obtain the optimal minimax strategy. This dual solution represents the "optimal strategy" of nature if the game were interpreted as a standard two-person zero sum game. We do not undertake such an interpretation or, rather, we prefer not to deduce any consequences from what might be called nature's "optimal strategies" since, in the context of reality, it does not seem reasonable to think of "nature" employing strategies fully symmetrical with those of the investor.

4.3
Interpretation of
Average Solutions

We have discussed the interpretations that can be offered for the solution to a particular game. Unfortunately, the solution to any one game rests on a variety of restrictive assumptions and simplifications. These specific characteristics reduce materially the normative significance of any single game, and they lead us to turn our attention to an average of the solutions to a number of games, representing a variety of plausible circumstances. In this section we attempt to interpret solutions averaged over a large number of experiments. In Figure 4-1 we present a histogram of the relative frequency with which each strategy is found to be optimal, as a proportion of the total number of 1014 experiments.[3] The relative frequencies are obtained by aggregating over all utility functions, Strategy Sets for nature, initial and final investor positions, and assumptions about the investor's tax liability. For purposes of this calculation, if a given pure strategy appears as a component of an optimal mixed strategy with a probability of, say 0.5, it is included in the average with a weight of $\frac{1}{2}$.

Perhaps the most remarkable characteristic of this summary is the extent to which strategies involving the use of options predominate over other possible stock market strategies. Even when the optimal strategy involves the purchase of stock, the investor is usually advised to combine his purchase with the writing of options. This result holds for all investor attitudes toward risk, with every decision criterion employed, and over all of nature's Strategy Sets. The reader will recall that our payoffs take into account both actual brokerage charges and dealer spreads between the premiums received and premiums paid for stock options. Optimal strategies involving options are fairly well divided between those involving buying and those involving writing, although option writing is more often an optimal strategy. Option-writing strategies are optimal in 53 per cent of the experiments whereas option buying is optimal only 39 per

---

[3] This is the number of experiments in which no interim trading was allowed. For a discussion of this latter assumption see Section 5.4.

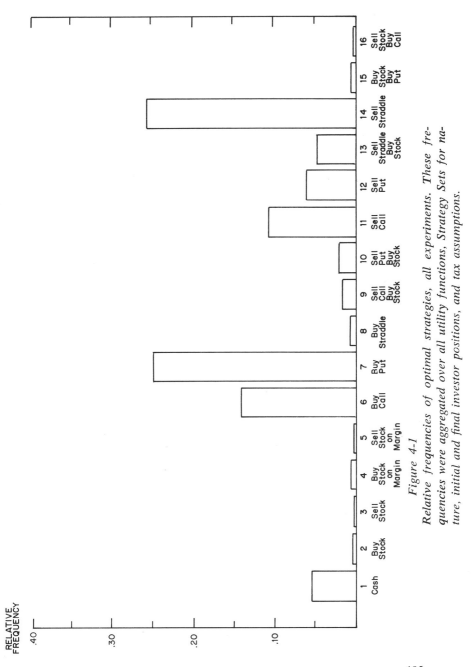

Figure 4-1

Relative frequencies of optimal strategies, all experiments. These frequencies were aggregated over all utility functions, Strategy Sets for nature, initial and final investor positions, and tax assumptions.

cent of the time.[4] Little support is found for the suggestions of some market practitioners, as noted in Chapter 2, that Strategies 15 and 16 involving the combination of Put or Call buying with long and short positions respectively would be useful investment strategies. It will be noted, however, that each of the sixteen strategies is optimal in some appropriate circumstances.

It appears from the figure that Put buying is preferable to Call buying. Such a conclusion is not warranted, however. The states of nature (future stock prices) used in all our experiments were evenly divided between those above and those below the stock price at the start of the holding period. Consequently, for an investor employing the Laplace criterion, the expected value of the stock price change over the 190-day holding period is zero. Of course, we depart from this assumption in certain experiments as, for example, when the +6 Strategy Set for nature is employed. But this is offset by the fact that the −6 Strategy Set is used an equal number of times. Thus the strategies of nature are assumed to be distributed symmetrically about a zero price change if we aggregate over all experiments. Since Puts are less costly than Calls, it follows that Put buying should more often be an optimal strategy, which is indeed what is reported in Figure 4-1. However, in practice investors believe the stock market has an upward secular trend, and thus it is clear that these 1014 experiments do not represent the average price expectations prevailing in the market. A similar argument applies to our interpretation of the meaning of the average of the solutions derived by solving games that employ different utility functions, since we assume investors have increasing marginal utility of money payoffs just as often as their utility functions are characterized by decreasing marginal utility. It is clear that the overall average solution in Figure 4-1 cannot be taken to indicate the relative frequencies with which we can expect various strategies to be undertaken in the real world if decision-makers act rationally.

Since the market appears to expect rising prices, it may be more relevant to examine a summary table of optimal strategies for all

---

[4] This result conflicts with the Katz conclusion reported in Chapter 1, footnote 32, that option selling was not a profitable strategy for a sample of transactions over a 21-month period from 1960 through 1962.

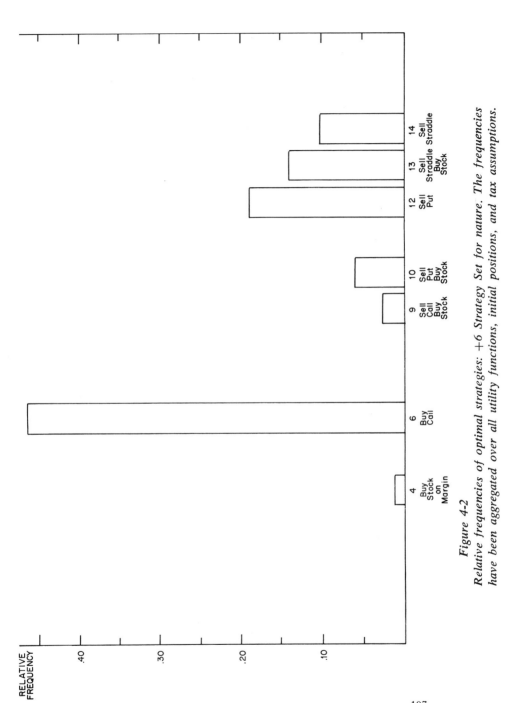

Figure 4-2
Relative frequencies of optimal strategies: +6 Strategy Set for nature. The frequencies have been aggregated over all utility functions, initial positions, and tax assumptions.

experiments performed under the assumption that the expected value of the stock price change is positive. Figure 4-2 presents the relative frequencies of optimal strategies for the subset of 300 experiments conducted with the +6 Strategy Set for nature. It will be noted that for these experiments Put buying is never an optimal strategy. As would be expected, the strategies most frequently optimal are Call buying and Put writing. There is also a considerable amount of stock buying in conjunction with option-writing strategies.

4.4
Interpretation of Changes in Optimal Solutions
as Circumstances Defining the Game Are Altered

In this section we analyze the changes in average optimal solutions that occur when particular circumstances defining the game are altered. The procedure will be to compare alternative solutions when a single characteristic of the game is varied. By this technique it will be possible to judge the effect on optimal strategy of the investor's tax status, his initial and final positions, and his attitude toward risk. In addition, it will be possible to analyze the role of the utility function and of the decision criterion employed by the investor. Such an analysis may help in both the choice of strategies most suitable for particular individuals and, ultimately, in developing rules for optimal investor behavior.

4.4.1   *Comparison of Optimal Strategies for the Cash-to-Cash*
and Stock-to-Stock Cases for a Tax-Exempt Investor

The cash-to-cash and stock-to-stock cases differ with respect to the initial and final positions of the investor and consequently in the amount of transactions costs involved in undertaking alternative strategies. In the cash-to-cash case the investor begins with a portfolio consisting entirely of cash and ends with a portfolio in which cash is the only asset. On the other hand, the stock-to-stock case assumes that the investor begins the period with a portfolio consisting of (100 shares of) common stock and ends with the identical securities.

A priori, we would expect the following differences between the two cases. Strategy 1, Cash, will involve two transactions costs in the stock-to-stock case, the cost of converting the individual's portfolio to cash (bonds) and the second cost of reinvesting his funds in stock at the end of the period. Conversely, there are no transactions costs involved in Strategy 1 for the cash-to-cash case. Consequently, we would expect that Strategy 1 would less frequently be an optimal strategy in the stock-to-stock case. For the same reasons, we would expect that strategies involving the buying of stock would be more likely to be optimal in the stock-to-stock case.

In Table 4-4 we present a summary showing the relative num-

Table 4-4

Relative Frequencies of Optimal Strategies[1]
Aggregated over All Utility Functions, Decision Criteria,
and Strategy Sets for Nature
(no dividends, tax-exempt investor)

	Cash Strategy	Strategies Involving Stock Buying and Option Writing	Strategies Involving Option Buying	Strategies Involving Option Writing Without Stock Buying
	1 Cash	2 BS	6 BC	11 SC
		9 SC,BS	7 BP	12 SP
		10 SP,BS		14 SSTR
		13 SSTR,BS		
Cash-to-Cash	.072	.057	.308	.562
Stock-to-Stock	.057	.138	.304	.500

[1] Strategies not explicitly listed in the column headings occur with zero frequency in all cases represented by this table.

ber of times each strategy is found to be optimal out of the total number of experiments performed. It will be noted that, as expected, the relative frequency of Strategy 1 (Cash) declines slightly from a relative frequency of .072 in the cash-to-cash case to a frequency of .057 in the other case, and the relative frequency of strategies involving stock buying increases in the stock-to-stock case.

In Table 4-5 we present a detailed comparison of behavior with different utility functions when the investor employs the minimax criterion and is tax-exempt. We note that for nature's +6 Strategy

Table 4-5

Comparison of Selected Minimax Cases for Tax-Exempt Investor (abstracting from dividends)

Utility Function	Minimax +6				Minimax 0			
	Cash-to-Cash		Stock-to-Stock		Cash-to-Cash		Stock-to-Stock	
	Strategy	Probability	Strategy	Probability	Strategy	Probability	Strategy	Probability
IMU 2.3	6 BC	.060	6 BC	.060	6 BC	.057	6 BC	.059
	12 SP	.610	12 SP	.622	7 BP	.031	7 BP	.031
	14 SSTR	.330	14 SSTR	.318	11 SC	.428	11 SC	.426
					12 SP	.483	12 SP	.484
CMU	12 SP	.782	13 SSTR,BS	.913	1 C	1.000	1 C	.995
	14 SSTR	.218	14 SSTR	.087			2 BS	.001
							9 SC,BS	.004
DMU 2.3	1 C	1.000	9 SC,BS	.988	1 C	1.000	1 C	1.000
			11 SC	.012				

Set, in the case of CMU and DMU utility functions, the change in assumptions regarding the investor's initial position changes the optimal strategy or strategies completely. In the stock-to-stock case, the optimal (mixed) strategies involve stock buying, with a probability over 0.9. It is interesting to note, however, that the change in assumptions makes almost no difference in the case of the IMU utility function. This appears to be so because the IMU utility function tends to augment the utility values of the extreme outcomes associated with levered strategies. A small change in transactions costs does not alter extreme payoffs sufficiently to change optimal strategies away from those involving Put and Call buying and option writing without a position in the stock.

4.4.2 Comparisons of Optimal Strategies for the Taxable and Tax-Exempt Investor

A priori, we would expect the introduction of personal income taxes to have the following general effect on the determination of optimal strategies: Those strategies for which the dollar returns are likely to be taxed at relatively high regular personal income tax rates will be optimal less frequently than those strategies whose dollar returns will be taxed at favorable capital gains rates. From this general observation it is easy to deduce a number of practical consequences.

The reader will recall from Chapter 2 that Strategy 1, Cash, (that is, investment in bonds) will tend to be optimal less often for the taxable investor because bond interest is taxed at regular personal income tax rates. The purchase of Put and Call options may be expected to be most heavily favored for the taxable investor, since returns from these strategies are treated as long-term capital gains when they are positive, and as short-term capital losses when they are negative.[5] Thus, under our particular assumptions, all gains are taxed at a 25 per cent rate, whereas losses are rebated at a 50 per

---

[5] The reader will recall from Chapter 2 that the investor is assumed to sell his option to a third party on the expiration date whenever a gain will be realized. This, in effect, makes all gains long-term capital gains for tax purposes. On the other hand, if the investor expects to realize a loss, he is assumed to sell his option to a third party for the nominal sum of one dollar prior to the end of the six-month holding period. Under our assumptions that the investor has offsetting short-term capital gains, this loss will, in effect, be rebated at regular personal income-tax rates.

cent rate.[6] For the same reasons, one would also expect the strategies of buying stock (and buying stock on margin) to be favored. If gains are realized, the securities will be sold after six months and long-term capital gains will be realized, in the cash-to-cash case. If losses occur, the securities will be sold before the end of the six-month holding period and the investor will realize a short-term capital loss. Finally, we would expect that strategies involving the writing of options would be optimal less frequently in the tax case. This is so because the premiums from writing options that are not exercised are treated as income or short-term capital gains for tax purposes.[7]

In Table 4-6 a summary comparison of relative frequency of optimal strategies for the tax and tax-exempt cases is presented. It will be seen that all of our a priori expectations are confirmed for the cash-to-cash experiments. The relative frequencies with which Put and Call buying appear as optimal strategies are 40.3 per cent for a taxable investor in contrast to 30.8 per cent for a tax-exempt investor. On the other hand, strategies involving the writing of options are less frequently optimal for taxable investors. It is worth noting that the introduction of personal income taxes removes some of the paradox from our earlier finding that option writing tended to be optimal more often than option buying. For the tax-exempt investor, option writing is an optimal strategy more than twice as frequently as option buying. In the case of a taxable investor, however, there is a much closer balance between the two types of strategies, although writing is still more prevalent. These comparisons suggest that tax-exempt financial institutions may find option writing particularly desirable. Finally, it should be noted that, as expected, stock buying alone appears as an optimal strategy for a taxable investor, whereas it was never optimal in the tax-exempt case.

---

[6] It should be noted, however, that if the investor has no offsetting capital gains, these losses may be deducted only up to a total of $1000. Thus, even for option buyers, the government's tax system would retain a "heads I win, tails you lose" bias against risk-taking under alternative assumptions about the amount of the investor's realized short-term gains.

[7] As we noted in Chapter 2, current Internal Revenue Service rules allow investors to treat the unexercised portion of a Straddle as a short-term capital gain rather than as income. Given our assumption that the investor does not have offsetting short-term capital losses, however, this ruling makes no difference in our results.

Table 4-6

Relative Frequencies of Optimal Strategies in Tax and Tax-Exempt Cases[1]
Aggregated over All Utility Functions, Decision Criteria, and Strategy Sets for Nature

		Cash Strategy	Strategies Involving Stock Buying	Strategies Involving Stock Buying and Option Writing	Strategies Involving Option Buying	Strategies Involving Option Writing Without Stock Buying
		1 Cash	2 BS 4 BSM	9 SC,BS 10 SP,BS 13 SSTR,BS	6 BC 7 BP	11 SC 12 SP 14 SSTR
Cash-to-Cash	Taxable Investor	.023	.057	.041	.403	.475
	Tax-Exempt Investor	.072	.000	.057	.308	.562
Stock-to-Stock	Taxable Investor	.025	.001	.116	.398	.459
	Tax-Exempt Investor	.057	.000	.138	.304	.500

[1] Strategies not explicitly listed in the column headings occur with zero frequency in all cases represented by this table.

In the stock-to-stock experiments we find that there is one exception to these findings. Strategies involving stock buying are actually less frequently optimal for a taxable investor than for one who is exempt from income taxes. The reason for this "anomaly" is that the tax effect is ambiguous or unfavorable to stock buying in the stock-to-stock experiments. It is true that when gains accrue, the taxable stock buyer does not realize these gains. In the cash-to-cash case these gains would be taxed at the capital gains rate, whereas in the present case there is no tax liability at all (at least within the holding period). On the other hand, under our assumptions realized losses established prior to the end of the six-month holding period (as in the cash-to-cash case) reduce the individual's income taxes by one half the amount of the loss. In the stock-to-stock case no losses are realized from long positions, and the individual forgoes this benefit. For all states of nature in which the stock price declines, the tax effect is, therefore, unfavorable in the stock-to-stock case.

It should be noted, however, that it is possible to introduce another tax effect that would increase the number of times that stock-buying strategies are considered optimal. If one assumed in the stock-to-stock case that the cost basis of the investor's stock is well below the market price at the start of the experiment period, there would be a penalty involved, beyond the transactions costs, in selling the stock. This penalty would be equal to the unrealized capital gain on the stock times the capital gains tax rate. The penalty could be avoided only by engaging in buying the stock at the start of the experiment period (i.e., holding on to the existing long position). We should emphasize, however, that when stock-buying strategies are optimal they usually occur in combination with some form of option writing. Thus it would appear that strategies involving option writing are optimal even for investors who are locked into their capital gains.

4.4.3 Comparisons of Investor's Optimal Strategies for Alternative Utility Functions

As was mentioned in Chapter 3, what is optimal from the point of view of an investor depends not only on the cash payoffs accruing to him but also upon the utility he derives therefrom. We experimented with utility functions that exhibited, in turn, increasing marginal utility of cash payoffs, decreasing marginal utility, and various types of composite and cubic utility functions. In this section the results of these experiments are discussed.

We turn first to a comparison of those utility functions exhibiting diminishing and increasing marginal utility. Such utility functions possess the general properties we associate with risk aversion and risk love, respectively. A priori, one would expect the investor whose utility function exhibits diminishing marginal utility (DMU) to choose relatively conservative strategies. On the other hand, the investor whose utility function exhibits increasing marginal utility (IMU) would be expected to opt for strategies that are in some sense more risky or more levered.

An examination of Tables 4-1, 4-2, and 4-3, which present results for the cash-to-cash, tax-exempt case, shows that our results are quite consistent with these expectations.[8] It should be noted that Strategy 1, Cash, the safest strategy, occurs most frequently as an optimal strategy under the assumption of DMU. On the other hand, Strategies 6 and 7, the purchase of Call and Put options respectively, which are among the most levered strategies, are most often optimal under the assumption of IMU. Interestingly, a change in the investor's attitude toward risk can turn an option writer into an option buyer. Note, for example, in Table 4-2, under the Hurwicz criterion (α = .50) and the −6 Strategy Set for nature, the risk-averse individual sells a Call and the risk lover buys a Put. While both strategies involve similar positions (see the vectors in Table 2-1), the purchase of a Put is a more levered strategy (see the payoffs in Table 3-2 not including the extended range). In general, as any market practitioner would have suggested, it is advisable for the investor to buy options whenever big price changes are expected, and for comparable reasons it is appropriate whenever he derives increasing marginal utility from money payoffs.

Other than these rather broad observations, it is difficult to interpret the differences in investors' optimal strategies for alternative utility functions, particularly where mixed optimal strategies are in-

---

[8] In the appendix to this chapter, Tables 4A-1 through 4A-7 present detailed results for a sample of other cases.

volved. For example, note the changes in optimal solutions for the alternative utility functions displayed in the first panel of Table 4-3 (minimax decision criterion). It is not easy to predict a priori which strategy numbers are likely to enter into the optimal strategy set when, for example, we move from linear utility to the utility functions involving IMU. In what sense can it be said that the optimal strategy set for IMU ($a = 2.3$) is "more risky" than the optimal strategy set for CMU? Such difficulties of interpretation lead us to a somewhat more sophisticated although still a rough criterion for the formulation of a priori expectations.

Consider the following two rankings of strategies: First, let us rank each strategy according to its worst dollar outcome from the point of view of the investor. We place at the top of the ranking that strategy for which the minimum payoff in dollars is the largest. We continue the sequence of strategies in order of descending minimum payoffs until we reach the bottom of the ranking, where we place that strategy for which the minimum payoff in dollars is the smallest. The second ranking is based on the best dollar outcomes. At the top of this list we place that strategy whose best outcome is most favorable from the viewpoint of the player. Continuing as for the first ranking, we place at the bottom of the list that strategy whose best outcome is least favorable to the player. We call the first of these two rankings the minimum payoff ranking. The second is labeled the maximum payoff ranking. The rankings for nature's 0 Strategy Set are shown in Table 4-7.

It will be helpful to refer to Figure 3-1 which displayed the utility functions for the decreasing and increasing marginal utility functions. How might we expect the optimal solutions for the cases of DMU and IMU to differ from the optimal solution for the linear utility case (CMU)? We note from Figure 3-1 that vis-à-vis CMU, the major effect of the DMU utility function is to make the disutility of losses (particularly the maximum loss) much greater than is the case for linear utility. The major effect of the IMU utility function, vis-à-vis the linear utility function, is to increase the utility value of big gains, particularly the maximum gain.

These observations, together with the rankings considered in the preceding paragraphs, can be used to make rather crude, but sur-

Table 4-7

**Ranking of Strategies According to
Minimum and Maximum Payoff**
(cash-to-cash: 0 Strategy Set for nature)

Tax-Exempt Case Ranking by Minimum Payoff	Taxable Case Ranking by Minimum Payoff	Tax-Exempt Case Ranking by Maximum Payoff	Taxable Case Ranking by Maximum Payoff
1 C	1 C	14 SSTR	14 SSTR
15 BS,BP	15 BS,BP	7 BP	7 BP
9 SC,BS; 16SS,BC	9 SC,BS; 16 SS,BC	6 BC; 11 SC	6 BC
2 BS; 3 SS	2 BS; 3 SS	12 SP	11 SC
13 SSTR,BS; 14 SSTR	13 SSTR,BS	10 SP,BS	12 SP
4 BSM	4 BSM; 5 SSM; 14 SSTR	4 BSM	4 BSM; 10 SP,BS
5 SSM	10 SP,BS	5 SSM	2 BS; 5 SSM; 13 SSTR,BS
10 SP,BS	11 SC	13 SSTR,BS	3 SS
11 SC	12 SP	2 BS; 3 SS	15 BS,BP
12 SP	6 BC; 7 BP; 8 BSTR	9 SC,BS	9 SC,BS
6 BC; 7 BP; 8 BSTR		15 BS,BP	8 BSTR
		16 SS,BC	16 SS,BC
		1 C	1 C
		8 BSTR	

prisingly reliable, predictions about the changes that might be expected in the optimal strategies from experiments performed with alternative utility functions. The rules of thumb employed were as follows:

1. When considering the effect of a change from the CMU to the IMU utility function (or when increasing the degree to which the IMU diverges from the CMU utility function) i.e., increasing the value of the parameter a, we would expect that if the optimal strategies change, they will change from strategy numbers lower in the maximum payoff ranking of Table 4-7 to numbers higher in the ranking.

2. When considering the effect of a change from the CMU to the DMU utility function (or when increasing the degree to which these two utility functions diverge from one another), i.e., increasing the value of the parameter a, we would expect that if the optimal

strategies change they will change from strategy numbers lower in the minimum payoff ranking of Table 4-7 to numbers higher in ranking.

These rules of thumb do have an intuitive explanation. Considering Rule 1 first, recall that the transformation from linear utility to increasing marginal utility has its greatest effect in altering the utility value of the maximum payoff for each strategy. The maximum payoff ranking runs from the least desirable maximum payoff (at the bottom) to the most desirable one (at the top). Therefore, as we increase the degree to which the marginal utility of gains increases, we would expect that any change in optimal strategy would be in the upward direction in the table. This is so because the strategies toward the top of the table will exhibit the greatest increase in utility value for the maximum payoffs. Relative to the case of linear utility, risk lovers (people whose marginal utility of gains increases) will tend to prefer strategies for which the maximum payoff is comparatively large.

It is true, of course, that all the payoffs change with the utility transformation, while the rule only looks at that outcome showing the biggest change. This is why we stress that our rule of thumb is merely a heuristic guide. We shall see in a moment, however, how good this guide turns out to be as a predictor.

The explanation of Rule 2 is completely analogous. The DMU utility function will have its greatest effect in altering the disutility value of the greatest loss for each strategy. The minimum payoff ranking of Table 4-7 has the strategy whose worst outcome is the most unfavorable at the bottom of the ranking and the strategy whose worst outcome is least undesirable at the top of the ranking. As utility is transformed, we would expect that to the extent an optimal strategy changes, the change will be in the direction of increasing the rank (desirability) of the optimal strategy. Relative to the case of the linear utility, risk averters (people whose marginal disutility of losses increases) will tend to prefer strategies where the maximum losses are relatively small.

We now illustrate how the rules of thumb operate in practice for a tax-exempt investor. The ranking of Table 4-7 and the results in Tables 4-8 and 4-9 will be used in this illustration. Recalling the rules of thumb, one would expect a change from linear utility to a utility function assuming diminishing marginal utility of money gains (increasing disutility of money losses) to have the following effect: To the extent optimal strategies changed, they would move from relatively low-ranked strategies in the minimum payoff ranking (Col-

Table 4-8

**Investor's Optimal Strategies for
Alternative Utility Functions**
(tax-exempt investor; cash-to-cash; 0 Strategy Set for nature)

Decision Criterion	IMU $a = 2.3$ Strategy	Proba- bility	CMU Strategy	Proba- bility	DMU $a = 2.3$ Strategy	Proba- bility
Minimax	6 BC	.057	1 C	1.000	1 C	1.000
	7 BP	.031				
	11 SC	.428				
	12 SP	.483				
Minimax Regret	7 BP	.230	1 C	.286	1 C	.701
	14 SSTR	.770	11 SC	.429	11 SC	.143
			14 SSTR	.285	14 SSTR	.156
Hurwicz $\alpha = .25$	14 SSTR	1.000	14 SSTR	1.000	14 SSTR	1.000
Hurwicz $\alpha = .50$	14 SSTR	1.000	14 SSTR	1.000	14 SSTR	1.000
Hurwicz $\alpha = .75$	14 SSTR	1.000	14 SSTR	1.000	14 SSTR	1.000
Laplace	14 SSTR	1.000	14 SSTR	1.000	14 SSTR	1.000

umn 1, Table 4-7) to relatively higher ranked strategies. We note in Table 4-8 that the optimal strategies change only when the minimax regret criterion is employed. Strategy 1, Cash, at the top of the minimum payoff ranking, is employed under the DMU function with a probability of .701, which is much higher than .286, the corresponding probability for the CMU function. Strategy 11, Sell Call, which is near the bottom of the ranking, is employed under the DMU function with a substantially lower probability than under the CMU function (.143 versus .429). Strategy 14, Sell Straddle, in the middle of the ranking, is employed with somewhat more comparable probabilities under the CMU and DMU functions.

In comparing the CMU with the IMU utility function, one would expect movement from lower to higher strategies in the maximum payoff ranking (Column 3 of Table 4-7). Employing the minimax criterion, Strategy 1, near the bottom of the ranking, is employed with a probability of 1.0 in the case of the CMU utility function. In the case of increasing marginal utility, however, four new strate-

Table 4-9

**Investor's Optimal Strategies for
Alternative IMU Utility Functions**
(tax-exempt investor; cash-to-cash; 0 Strategy Set for nature)

Selected Values of a in IMU Utility Function[1]	Minimax Regret Decision Criterion Strategy	Probability
2.3	7 BP	.230
	14 SSTR	.770
1.6	7 BP	.290
	14 SSTR	.710
1.0	7 BP	.328
	14 SSTR	.672
0.8	11 SC	.611
	12 SP	.017
	14 SSTR	.373
0.6	11 SC	.619
	12 SP	.086
	14 SSTR	.297
0.4	1 C	.213
	11 SC	.474
	14 SSTR	.313
0.0 (CMU utility function)	1 C	.286
	11 SC	.429
	14 SSTR	.285

[1] The role of the parameter a in the IMU utility function is given in the formula $U(x) = (x + e^{ax} - 1)/e^a$. See Section 3.1.

gies become optimal, all of which are higher in the ranking table. For the minimax regret criterion, the decision-maker moves out of Strategies 1 and 11 (employed in the CMU case) and into Strategies 7 and 14 (for the IMU utility function). The latter two strategies are both higher in the maximum payoff ranking than the former two strategies. These changes are fully consistent with those anticipated by the use of the rules of thumb. In comparing the CMU with the DMU function one may note for the minimax regret criterion a preponderant shift to Strategy 1, which is the highest-ranked strategy in the minimum payoff rankings. This is again as expected on a priori grounds.

It is also interesting to consider how the optimal strategies change as small changes are made in the coefficient a, which regulates the degree to which the IMU or DMU utility functions diverge from the CMU utility function. In Table 4-9, the optimal strategies under the minimax regret criterion and IMU utility function are shown for alternative values of a. With an a value of 0 (the linear utility case) the optimal strategies are numbers 1, 11, and 14. When the value of a is increased to 0.4, Strategy 14, the highest strategy in the table of rankings by maximum payoff (Table 4-7), increases in probability and Strategy 1, one of the lowest strategies in the maximum payoff rankings, decreases in probability. Increasing the value of a to 0.6 causes Strategy 1 to drop out and to be replaced by Strategy 12, much higher up in the maximum payoff ranking. When the value of a is further increased to 0.8, Strategy 14, the highest-ranked strategy, is employed with a larger probability, while the probability numbers associated with (lower-ranked) Strategies 11 and 12 decline. When a reaches a value of unity, Strategies 11 and 12 are no longer optimal and Strategy 7, the second highest strategy in the ranking table becomes an optimal strategy. As a is further increased, Strategy 7 is employed to a smaller extent and Strategy 14, the highest-ranked strategy, is used to an increasing extent.

For readers who would like to continue this exercise, we furnish in Tables 4A-8 and 4A-9 in the appendix to this chapter minimum and maximum payoff rankings for nature's $+6$ and -6 Strategy Sets. Tables 4-1 through 4-3 and 4A-1 through 4A-3 may be used to find how the optimal strategies change with alternative utility functions.

We turn next to an examination of the two composite utility functions. The first, called Composite IMU, has increasing marginal utility of gains and increasing marginal disutility of losses. The second, called Composite DMU, has decreasing marginal utility of

Table 4-10

Utility Functions Exhibiting Increasing and Decreasing Marginal Utility of Gains and Disutility of Losses
(tax-exempt case; cash-to-cash; 0 Strategy Set for nature)

Decision Criterion	Composite IMU a = 2.3[1] Strategy	Probability	CMU Strategy	Probability	Composite DMU a = 2.3 Strategy	Probability	Ranking by Sum of Minimum and Maximum Outcomes
Minimax	1 C	1.000	1 C	1.000	1 C	1.000	14 SSTR 1 C
Minimax Regret	7 BP 14 SSTR	.205 .795	1 C 11 SC 14 SSTR	.286 .429 .285	1 C 11 SC 12 SP	.288 .495 .216	7 BP 9 SC,BS; 15 BS,BP 2 BS; 3 SS; 11 SC 16 SS,BC
Hurwicz α = .25	14 SSTR	1.000	14 SSTR	1.000	1 C	1.000	4 BSM; 5 SSM
Hurwicz α = .50	14 SSTR	1.000	14 SSTR	1.000	14 SSTR	1.000	10 SP,BS
Hurwicz α = .75	14 SSTR	1.000	14 SSTR	1.000	14 SSTR	1.000	13 SSTR,BS 12 SP
Laplace	14 SSTR	1.000	14 SSTR	1.000	14 SSTR	1.000	6 BC 8 BSTR

[1] The number 2.3 refers to the value of the parameter a in equations (3.2) and (3.3).

gains and disutility of losses. Examples of the two utility functions are depicted in Figure 3-2, page 80.

It will be seen from the figure that, relative to the CMU utility function, the investor with a Composite IMU utility function will be better off with relatively large gains and small losses. On the other hand, the investor with a Composite DMU utility function is worse off relative to the investor with the CMU utility function when gains are big and losses are small. Needless to say, we do not mean to imply that such a utility function is in any sense realistic. Our interest is simply in examining the changes in investors' optimal strategies that result from altering the assumptions about utility surfaces.

The ranking tables constructed for these cases were calculated by taking the sums of the best and worst outcomes for each available strategy. The strategy with the highest algebraic sum appears at the top of the ranking. The optimal strategies for an investor with a Composite IMU utility function will presumably tend to move up the ranking table vis-à-vis the CMU solution. This is so because a higher ranking means that gains tend to be big and losses small. The situation is just the opposite for an investor with a Composite DMU utility function, since he is better off, relative to the linear utility case, with small gains and big losses. Thus we suggest that changing from a linear to a Composite DMU utility function will cause the optimal strategies to shift down in the ranking table.

Table 4-10 presents both the experiments and the composite ranking table. It will be noticed that all of the changes are in the direction hypothesized. Optimal strategies tend to move up (down) the ranking table when the utility function is transformed from linear to Composite IMU (DMU) utility. Experiments were also conducted with the cubic utility function, $U(x) = x^3$. As can be seen from Figure 3-2, this function is very similar to the Composite IMU utility function. It is not surprising, therefore, that the optimal solutions for "cubic" utility were essentially the same as for Composite IMU utility.

4.4.4 Comparisons of Investor's Optimal Strategies for Alternative Decision Criteria

Of all the "circumstances" that jointly define a particular game or experiment, we found it hardest to interpret the significance of the particular decision criterion employed by the investor. Whereas the meaning of the investor's initial position or of the shape of his utility function can be grasped intuitively with little or no difficulty, the differences among the various decision criteria can be argued only in terms of (1) the set of mathematical axioms consistent with the criteria or (2) the consequences (in particular choice situations) of their application. Their intuitive meaning and an understanding of their *general* consequences continue to remain somewhat elusive.

Certain things are, of course, well known about the various decision criteria. Such items are the observation that the minimax criterion is peculiarly pessimistic, that the Hurwicz criterion coincides with the minimax criterion for $\alpha = 0$ if mixed strategies are ruled out, and that each of the major criteria violates one or more desirable axioms. But it is not clear why a person should transform the matrix of payoffs into a matrix of regrets before he applies the minimax criterion; nor is it clear that, once he has transformed the matrix into a regret matrix, the only sensible thing to do is to apply the minimax criterion. Specifically, why not employ a Hurwicz criterion in conjunction with a regret matrix? Of course, such a new decision criterion also violates some axioms[9] but seems intuitively no less sensible than minimax regret.

For these reasons it is difficult to suggest a priori as many clear-cut results as in the cases when some other characteristic of the game was varied. However, some analysis of the effects of employing different decision criteria can still be carried out, and this is the objective of the present section.

We remarked earlier that the utility function of the investor and the decision criterion he chooses are logically independent. The former assigns utility or a satisfaction level to events and is independent of the subjective (or objective) probabilities associated with events. The latter reflects the individual's views concerning the ease or difficulty of realizing various events. Nevertheless, certain utility functions may lead the investor to choose the same types of strategies that may be implied by particular decision criteria. For example, risk aversion, as indicated by the sign of $U''(x)$, is frequently associated with "conservative" behavior in some sense. The minimax criterion

---

[9] Namely the axioms of row adjunction and convexity.

Table 4-11

Relative Frequencies of Optimal Strategies Aggregated over All Experiments

Decision Criteria and Utility Function	Strategies															
	1	2	3	4	5	6	7	8	9	10	11	12	13	14	15	16
Minimax IMU $a = 2.3$						.039	.036				.314	.366		.244		
Hurwicz $\alpha = .75$ DMU $a = 2.3$									.167	.333	.167		.333			
Minimax DMU $a = 2.3$	.333	.022							.309		.261		.075			
Hurwicz $\alpha = .75$ IMU $a = 2.3$						.333	.333								.333	

is thought to reflect a pessimistic view of nature and thus to imply conservative behavior too. This suggests that a conservative utility function may to some extent compensate for a less conservative decision criterion.

We found that this type of compensation does occur to some extent. In Table 4-11 we present the relative frequencies of optimal strategies for certain pairs of decision criteria and utility functions. In the first row of the table the conservative minimax strategy is coupled with the risk-loving IMU utility function. In the second row the optimistic Hurwicz criterion ($\alpha = .75$) is combined with the risk-averse DMU utility function. A comparison of the two rows may be expected to reveal that the combinations tend to yield similar optimal strategies. On the other hand, combining the pessimistic minimax criterion with the risk-averse DMU utility function (row 3) and the optimistic Hurwicz criterion with the risk-loving IMU utility function (row 4) should accentuate the differences between the decision criteria.

In order to perform these pairwise comparisons we shall judge the closeness to each other or the similarity of two strategies by the (square of the) Euclidean distance between the two 16-element vectors representing the strategies. That is to say, if a_i and b_i ($i = 1, \ldots, 16$) represent the elements of the two rows to be compared, our criterion of similarity is $D^2 = \Sigma_{i=1}^{16} (a_i - b_i)^2$. The value of D^2 is .468 for rows 1 and 2 and .613 for rows 3 and 4, confirming our conjecture. As a matter of fact, as the table indicates, there is no overlap at all in the optimal strategies for rows 3 and 4. A conservative criterion and risk-loving utility function tend to produce results similar to those obtained with a less conservative criterion and risk-averse utility function. Thus although the strength of this influence may be only moderate, a risk-loving utility function can compensate for a conservative decision criterion.

Several other findings can be ascertained from Table 4-12 in which we display the average strategies for each decision criterion, with aggregation of games over all standard-range, tax-exempt, and cash-to-cash experiments. For example, if we compute the appropriate D^2 values we find that the minimax criterion yields results that are better approximated by the Hurwicz criterion with $\alpha = .25$ than

Table 4-12

Relative Frequencies of Optimal Strategies Aggregated over All Cash-to-Cash Experiments

Decision Criterion	1	2	3	4	5	6	7	8	9	10	11	12	13	14	15	16
									Strategies							
Minimax	.267		.004			.008	.018		.062		.239	.183	.068	.151		
Minimax Regret	.068					.090	.197				.205	.135	.046	.260		
Hurwicz $\alpha = .25$	.100					.133	.167				.167	.033	.167	.233		
Hurwicz $\alpha = .50$						.233	.267				.067	.100		.333		
Hurwicz $\alpha = .75$						.267	.300				.033	.067		.333		
Laplace							.167				.167	.167		.500		

127

by the other two Hurwicz criteria (.114 versus .276 and .312 respectively). We also find that the three Hurwicz criteria produce results that are quite similar to one another. The minimax criterion is closer to the minimax regret criterion than to any other — a finding that seems difficult to explain. We observe also that the results of the Hurwicz criteria, the Laplace criterion, and the minimax regret criterion are all relatively close to each other and that the largest distances between pairs of average solution vectors always involve the minimax criterion.[10] We also note the reasonable result that with the relatively pessimistic criteria such as minimax, Hurwicz with $\alpha = .25$, and minimax regret there is relatively more holding of cash than with the more optimistic Hurwicz criteria ($\alpha = .50$ and .75), while the latter lead to more purchasing of options (Strategies 6, 7, and 14). We finally observe that all the decision criteria produce roughly similar results in that Strategies 2, 3, 4, 5, 8, 9, 10, 15, and 16 appear in negligible amounts only, if at all, and that strategies involving the use of options are prevalent irrespective of the decision criterion employed.

Although it is possible to report more findings of this type and more such comparisons, they all tend to be less clear-cut and harder to interpret than the ones discussed in previous sections. We feel that a fundamental reason for this is the difficulty of providing a strong intuitive basis for the nature of the various decision criteria.

4.4.5 Comparisons of Optimal Strategies for Dividend and Nondividend Cases

In our previous results we have abstracted entirely from the payment of dividends. It is desirable that at least one set of experiments be devoted to an investigation of the effects of the payment of corporate dividends. We performed these computations only for the stock-to-stock case, assuming the payment of personal income taxes. We assumed that an annual dividend rate of 3.2 per cent would be paid by the typical $50 stock. This rate is roughly in line with average dividends paid on common shares during the 1960–1964 period.

---

[10] The comparison of minimax and Laplace yields $D^2 = .229$, minimax and Hurwicz with $\alpha = .50$ yields $D^2 = .276$ and finally, minimax and Hurwicz with $\alpha = .75$ yields $D^2 = .312$.

During the six-month ten-day holding period, we assumed the dividends would be paid at the rate of 1.6 per cent.

A priori, we would expect that dividend payments would tend to make long positions in common stock more desirable (since the holder would receive the dividends) and would tend to discourage the use of short positions (since these strategies would involve the payment of dividends). The situation is slightly more complex for strategies involving Puts and Calls. The buyer of a Call option tends to get the dividend only if the Call is exercised (that is, if the price goes up). Thus, we would expect that dividend payments would especially favor strategies involving the buying of Call options for the +6 Strategy Set of nature, where for most of the outcomes the Call would be exercised. The buyer of a Put option pays the dividend only in the case of the option being exercised (that is, if the price goes down). Consequently, we would expect that Put-buying strategies would be most discouraged in the −6 Strategy Set of nature, where most of the outcomes involve lower stock prices. Similar a priori expectations for strategies involving option writing and for various combination strategies may be easily derived from Table 2-2, which indicates how dividends affect the pay-offs.

The results of our experiments confirm all our a priori expectations. Wherever there are changes in the optimal strategies, the direction of change is always as anticipated. However, it should be noted that in most cases optimal strategies were unchanged by the payment of dividends. Where mixed strategies were employed, the probabilities associated with these strategies tended to change very slightly. We conclude that the introduction of dividend payments would alter our tables of results only inconsequentially.

4.4.6 Comparisons of the Standard-Range and Extended-Range Strategy Sets for Nature

One final set of comparisons will be presented. Table 4-13 compares the average solutions for the standard range with those for the extended-range Strategy Sets for nature. A priori, one would expect that the greater is the possible range of future stock prices, the more attractive is option buying relative to option writing. Comparing rows 1 and 2 of the table, this conjecture is supported. In the standard-

Table 4-13

Extended-Range and Standard-Range
Strategy Sets for Nature
Relative Frequencies of Optimal Strategies[1]
Aggregated over All Utility Functions and Decision Criteria
(cash-to-cash case; tax-exempt investor)

	Cash Strategy	Strategies Involving Option Selling		Strategies Involving Option Buying	
		9 SC,BS 11 SC		6 BC 15 BS,BP	
	1 Cash	10 SP,BS 12 SP		7 BP 16 SS,BC	
		13 SSTR,BS 14 SSTR		8 BSTR	
Standard-Range Strategy Set (Aggregated over +6, 0, and −6 Strategy Sets)	.072	.619		.308	
Extended-Range Strategy Set: Standard Premium	.071	.057		.867	
Extended-Range Strategy Set: Nonstandard Premium	.220	.057		.723	

[1] Strategies not explicitly listed in the column headings occur with zero or negligible frequency in all cases represented by this table.

range case, option selling is optimal twice as often as option buying. In the extended-range case, however, option buying is overwhelmingly an optimal strategy, although it becomes somewhat less so with introduction of the nonstandard (i.e., larger) premium.

Appendix

Table 4A-1

**Investor's Optimal Strategies for Alternative
Utility Functions and Strategy Sets for Nature**
(cash-to-cash case; taxable investor)

Minimax and Minimax Regret Criteria;
Vary Risk Attitude and Distribution

Risk Attitude	Minimax +6 Strategy	Proba-bility	Minimax 0 Strategy	Proba-bility	Minimax −6 Strategy	Proba-bility
IMU 2.3[1]	6 BC	.131	4 BSM	.465		
	12 SP	.443	7 BP	.037	7 BP	.164
	14 SSTR	.426	11 SC	.342	11 SC	.287
			12 SP	.156	14 SSTR	.549
CMU	4 BSM	.725	4 BSM	.662	7 BP	.308
	14 SSTR	.275	7 BP	.056	14 SSTR	.691
			11 SC	.283		
DMU 2.3	11 SC	.961	1 C	1.000	11 SC	.883
	14 SSTR	.039			14 SSTR	.117
	Minimax Regret +6		Minimax Regret 0		Minimax Regret −6	
IMU 2.3	6 BC	.702	7 BP	.467	7 BP	.898
	14 SSTR	.298	14 SSTR	.533	14 SSTR	.102
CMU	6 BC	.235	4 BSM	.232	7 BP	.656
	12 SP	.765	7 BP	.019	14 SSTR	.344
			11 SC	.748		
DMU 2.3	4 BSM	.128	1 C	.665	7 BP	.212
	6 BC	.080	9 SC,BS	.032	11 SC	.788
	12 SP	.793	11 SC	.303		

Table 4A-1 (continued)

Laplace and Hurwicz Criteria;
Vary Risk Attitude and Distribution

Risk Attitude	Laplace			Hurwicz $\alpha = .25$		
	+6	0	−6	+6	0	−6
IMU 2.3	6 BC	14 SSTR	7 BP	6 BC	14 SSTR	7 BP
CMU	12 SP	14 SSTR	7 BP	13 SSTR,BS	14 SSTR	11 SC
DMU 2.3	12 SP	14 SSTR	11 SC	13 SSTR,BS	1 C	11 SC
	Hurwicz $\alpha = .50$			Hurwicz $\alpha = .75$		
IMU 2.3	6 BC	14 SSTR	7 BP	6 BC	14 SSTR	7 BP
CMU	6 BC	14 SSTR	7 BP	6 BC	14 SSTR	7 BP
DMU 2.3	4 BSM	14 SSTR	11 SC	6 BC	14 SSTR	7 BP

[1] The number 2.3 refers to the value of the parameter a in equations (3.2) and (3.3).

Table 4A-2

Investor's Optimal Strategies for Alternative Decision Criteria and Utility Functions
(cash-to-cash case; taxable investor)

Decision Criterion	IMU Strategy	IMU 2.3¹ Probability	CMU Strategy	CMU Probability	DMU Strategy	DMU 2.3 Probability
Distribution +6. Vary Risk Attitude and Decision Criterion						
Minimax	6 BC	.131	4 BSM	.725	11 SC	.961
	12 SP	.443	14 SSTR	.275	14 SSTR	.039
	14 SSTR	.426				
Minimax Regret	6 BC	.702	6 BC	.235	4 BSM	.128
	14 SSTR	.298	12 SP	.765	6 BC	.080
					12 SP	.793
Hurwicz $\alpha = .25$	6 BC	1.000	13 SSTR,BS	1.000	13 SSTR,BS	1.000
Hurwicz $\alpha = .50$	6 BC	1.000	6 BC	1.000	4 BSM	1.000
Hurwicz $\alpha = .75$	6 BC	1.000	6 BC	1.000	6 BC	1.000
Laplace	6 BC	1.000	12 SP	1.000	12 SP	1.000
Distribution 0. Vary Risk Attitude and Decision Criterion						
Minimax	4 BSM	.465	4 BSM	.662	1 C	1.000
	7 BP	.037	7 BP	.056		
	11 SC	.342	11 SC	.283		
	12 SP	.156				
Minimax Regret	7 BP	.465	4 BSM	.233	1 C	.665
	14 SSTR	.533	7 BP	.019	9 SC,BS	.032
			11 SC	.748	11 SC	.303

(continued on page 134)

Table 4A-2 (continued)

Hurwicz $\alpha = .25$	14 SSTR	1.000	14 SSTR	1.000	1 C	1.000
Hurwicz $\alpha = .50$	14 SSTR	1.000	14 SSTR	1.000	14 SSTR	1.000
Hurwicz $\alpha = .75$	14 SSTR	1.000	14 SSTR	1.000	14 SSTR	1.000
Laplace	14 SSTR	1.000	14 SSTR	1.000	14 SSTR	1.000
Distribution −6. Vary Risk Attitude and Decision Criterion — Minimax	7 BP	.164	7 BP	.308	11 SC	.883
	11 SC	.287	14 SSTR	.691	14 SSTR	.117
	14 SSTR	.549				
Minimax Regret	7 BP	.898	7 BP	.656	7 BP	.212
	14 SSTR	.102	14 SSTR	.344	11 SC	.788
Hurwicz $\alpha = .25$	7 BP	1.000	11 SC	1.000	11 SC	1.000
Hurwicz $\alpha = .50$	7 BP	1.000	7 BP	1.000	11 SC	1.000
Hurwicz $\alpha = .75$	7 BP	1.000	7 BP	1.000	7 BP	1.000
Laplace	7 BP	1.000	7 BP	1.000	11 SC	1.000

[1] The number 2.3 refers to the value of the parameter a in equations (3.2) and (3.3).

Table 4A-3

Investor's Optimal Strategies for Extended-Range Strategy Set

(cash-to-cash case; taxable investor)

Decision Criterion	IMU 2.3[2] Strategy	Proba-bility	IMU 1.6 Strategy	Proba-bility	CMU Strategy	Proba-bility	DMU 1.6 Strategy	Proba-bility	DMU 2.3 Strategy	Proba-bility
Minimax	4 BSM	.537	4 BSM	.594	7 BP	.027	1 C	1.000	1 C	1.000
	7 BP	.026	7 BP	.040	9 SC,BS	.276				
	11 SC	.355	11 SC	.328	11 SC	.146				
	12 SP	.082	12 SP	.038	15 BS,BP	.551				
Minimax Regret	6 BC	.064	6 BC	.136	6 BC	.428	7 BP	.151	8 BSTR	.433
	7 BP	.936	7 BP	.864	7 BP	.572	8 BSTR	.586	7 BP	.119
							16 SS,BC	.264	16 SS,BC	.448
Hurwicz α = .25	7 BP	1.000	7 BP	1.000	7 BP	1.000	15 BS,BP	1.000	15 BS,BP	1.000
Hurwicz α = .50	7 BP	1.000	7 BP	1.000	7 BP	1.000	7 BP	1.000	7 BP	1.000
Hurwicz α = .75	7 BP	1.000	7 BP	1.000	7 BP	1.000	7 BP	1.000	7 BP	1.000
Laplace	7 BP	1.000	7 BP	1.000	7 BP	1.000	8 BSTR	1.000	8 BSTR	1.000
Maximum Expected Utility Based on Posterior Distribution[1]	7 BP	1.000	7 BP	1.000	14 SSTR	1.000	9 SC,BS	1.000	9 SC,BS	1.000

Risk Level

[1] See Section 5.1 for a description of the posterior distribution employed.

[2] The numbers 2.3 and 1.6 refer to the values of parameter a in equations (3.2) and (3.3).

Table 4A-4

Investor's Optimal Strategies for Alternative Utility Functions and Strategy Sets for Nature, Tax-Exempt Investor (stock-to-stock case)

Minimax and Minimax Regret Decision Criteria

Utility Function	Minimax +6		Minimax 0		Minimax −6	
	Strategy	Proba-bility	Strategy	Proba-bility	Strategy	Proba-bility
IMU 2.3[1]	6 BC	.060	6 BC	.059	7 BP	.079
	12 SP	.622	7 BP	.031	11 SC	.509
	14 SSTR	.318	11 SC	.426	14 SSTR	.411
			12 SP	.484		
CMU	13 SSTR,BS	.913	1 C	.995	11 SC	.798
	14 SSTR	.087	2 BS	.001	14 SSTR	.202
			9 SC,BS	.004		
DMU 2.3	9 SC,BS	.988	1 C	1.000	11 SC	.771
	11 SC	.011			13 SSTR,BS	.229
	Minimax Regret +6		Minimax Regret 0		Minimax Regret −6	
IMU 2.3	6 BC	.506	7 BP	.239	7 BP	.862
	14 SSTR	.494	14 SSTR	.761	14 SSTR	.138
CMU	6 BC	.002	9 SC,BS	.265	7 BP	.245
	12 SP	.998	11 SC	.489	11 SC	.755
			14 SSTR	.246		
DMU 2.3	10 SP,BS	.043	9 SC,BS	.739	7 BP	.055
	12 SP	.418	11 SC	.253	11 SC	.945
	13 SSTR,BS	.539	14 SSTR	.008		

Laplace and Hurwicz Decision Criteria

Utility Function	Laplace			Hurwicz $\alpha = .25$		
	+6	0	−6	+6	0	−6
IMU 2.3	14 SSTR	14 SSTR	7 BP	6 BC	14 SSTR	7 BP
CMU	12 SP	14 SSTR	11 SC	13 SSTR,BS	14 SSTR	11 SC
DMU 2.3	12 SP	14 SSTR	11 SC	13 SSTR,BS	1 C	11 SC
	Hurwicz $\alpha = .50$			Hurwicz $\alpha = .75$		
IMU 2.3	6 BC	14 SSTR	7 BP	6 BC	14 SSTR	7 BP
CMU	6 BC	14 SSTR	7 BP	6 BC	14 SSTR	7 BP
DMU 2.3	10 SP,BS	14 SSTR	11 SC	10 SP,BS	14 SSTR	11 SC

[1] The number 2.3 refers to the value of the parameter a in equations (3.2) and (3.3).

Table 4A-5

Investor's Optimal Strategies for Alternative Utility Functions and Strategy Sets for Nature, Taxable Investor (stock-to-stock case)

Minimax and Minimax Regret Criteria;
Vary Risk Attitude and Distribution

Risk Attitude	Minimax +6		Minimax 0		Minimax −6	
	Strategy	Probability	Strategy	Probability	Strategy	Probability
IMU 2.3[1]	6 BC	.050	7 BP	.043	7 BP	.171
	10 SP,BS	.528	10 SP,BS	.493	11 SC	.203
	14 SSTR	.422	11 SC	.410	14 SSTR	.566
			13 SSTR,BS	.055		
CMU	13 SSTR,BS	.749	7 BP	.095	7 BP	.306
	14 SSTR	.251	9 SC,BS	.708	14 SSTR	.694
			11 SC	.196		
DMU 2.3	9 SC,BS	.877	1 C	.998	11 SC	.880
	14 SSTR	.123	9 SC,BS	.002	14 SSTR	.120
			14 SSTR	.0001		
	Minimax Regret +6		Minimax Regret 0		Minimax Regret −6	
IMU 2.3	6 BC	.718	7 BP	.470	7 BP	.898
	14 SSTR	.282	14 SSTR	.530	14 SSTR	.102
CMU	6 BC	.254	7 BP	.046	7 BP	.656
	12 SP	.746	9 SC, BS	.262	14 SSTR	.344
			11 SC	.691		
DMU 2.3	10 SP,BS	.592	1 C	.709	7 BP	.212
	12 SP	.408	11 SC	.291	11 SC	.788
			14 SSTR	.001		

Laplace and Hurwicz Criteria;
Vary Risk Attitude and Distribution

Risk Attitude	Laplace			Hurwicz α = .25		
	+6	0	−6	+6	0	−6
IMU 2.3	6 BC	14 SSTR	7 BP	6 BC	14 SSTR	7 BP
CMU	12 SP	14 SSTR	7 BP	13 SSTR,BS	14 SSTR	11 SC
DMU 2.3	12 SP	14 SSTR	11 SC	9 SC,BS	1 C	11 SC
	Hurwicz α = .50			Hurwicz α = .75		
IMU 2.3	6 BC	14 SSTR	7 BP	6 BC	14 SSTR	7 BP
CMU	6 BC	14 SSTR	7 BP	6 BC	14 SSTR	7 BP
DMU 2.3	13 SSTR,BS	14 SSTR	11 SC	6 BC	14 SSTR	7 BP

[1] The number 2.3 refers to the value of the parameter a in equations (3.2) and (3.3).

Table 4A-6

Investor's Optimal Strategies for Composite IMU Utility Function, Cash-to-Cash
$(a = 2.3)$[1]

Tax-Exempt Investor

Decision Criterion	+6 Strategy Set Strategy	Proba-bility	0 Strategy Set Strategy	Proba-bility	−6 Strategy Set Strategy	Proba-bility
Minimax	13 SSTR,BS	.970	1 C	1.000	7 BP	.070
	14 SSTR	.030			11 SC	.474
					14 SSTR	.456
Minimax Regret	6 BC	.559	7 BP	.205	7 BP	.845
	14 SSTR	.441	14 SSTR	.795	14 SSTR	.155
Hurwicz $\alpha = .25$	6 BC	1.000	14 SSTR	1.000	7 BP	1.000
Hurwicz $\alpha = .50$	6 BC	1.000	14 SSTR	1.000	7 BP	1.000
Hurwicz $\alpha = .75$	6 BC	1.000	14 SSTR	1.000	7 BP	1.000
Laplace	14 SSTR	1.000	14 SSTR	1.000	7 BP	1.000

Taxable Investor

Decision Criterion	+6 Strategy Set Strategy	Proba-bility	0 Strategy Set Strategy	Proba-bility	−6 Strategy Set Strategy	Proba-bility
Minimax	6 BC	.188	4 BSM	.682	7 BP	.116
	12 SP	.287	7 BP	.028	11 SC	.311
	14 SSTR	.524	11 SC	.290	14 SSTR	.573
Minimax Regret	6 BC	.696	7 BP	.424	7 BP	.884
	14 SSTR	.304	14 SSTR	.576	14 SSTR	.116
Hurwicz $\alpha = .25$	6 BC	1.000	14 SSTR	1.000	7 BP	1.000
Hurwicz $\alpha = .50$	6 BC	1.000	14 SSTR	1.000	7 BP	1.000
Hurwicz $\alpha = .75$	6 BC	1.000	14 SSTR	1.000	7 BP	1.000
Laplace	6 BC	1.000	14 SSTR	1.000	7 BP	1.000

[1] The number 2.3 refers to the value of the parameter a in equations (3.2) and (3.3).

Table 4A-7

Investor's Optimal Strategies for Composite IMU Utility Function, Stock-to-Stock $(a = 2.3)$[1]

Tax-Exempt Investor

Decision Criterion	+6 Strategy Set		0 Strategy Set		−6 Strategy Set	
	Strategy	Probability	Strategy	Probability	Strategy	Probability
Minimax	6 BC	.060	6 BC	.059	7 BP	.079
	12 SP	.622	7 BP	.031	11 SC	.510
	14 SSTR	.318	11 SC	.426	14 SSTR	.411
			12 SP	.484		
Minimax Regret	6 BC	.506	7 BP	.239	7 BP	.862
	14 SSTR	.494	14 SSTR	.761	14 SSTR	.138
Hurwicz $\alpha = .25$	6 BC	1.000	14 SSTR	1.000	7 BP	1.000
Hurwicz $\alpha = .50$	6 BC	1.000	14 SSTR	1.000	7 BP	1.000
Hurwicz $\alpha = .75$	6 BC	1.000	14 SSTR	1.000	7 BP	1.000
Laplace	14 SSTR	1.000	14 SSTR	1.000	7 BP	1.000

Taxable Investor

Decision Criterion	+6 Strategy Set		0 Strategy Set		−6 Strategy Set	
	Strategy	Probability	Strategy	Probability	Strategy	Probability
Minimax	6 BC	.050	7 BP	.043	7 BP	.171
	10 SP,BS	.528	10 SP,BS	.493	11 SC	.263
	14 SSTR	.422	11 SC	.410	14 SSTR	.566
			13 SSTR,BS	.055		
Minimax Regret	6 BC	.718	7 BP	.470	7 BP	.898
	14 SSTR	.282	14 SSTR	.530	14 SSTR	.102
Hurwicz $\alpha = .25$	6 BC	1.000	14 SSTR	1.000	7 BP	1.000
Hurwicz $\alpha = .50$	6 BC	1.000	14 SSTR	1.000	7 BP	1.000
Hurwicz $\alpha = .75$	6 BC	1.000	14 SSTR	1.000	7 BP	1.000
Laplace	6 BC	1.000	14 SSTR	1.000	7 BP	1.000

[1] The number 2.3 refers to the value of the parameter a in equations (3.2) and (3.3).

Table 4A-8

Ranking of Strategies According to Minimum and Maximum Payoff, −6 Strategy Set for Nature
(cash-to-cash)

Tax-Exempt Case Ranking by Minimum Payoff	Taxable Case Ranking by Minimum Payoff	Tax-Exempt Case Ranking by Maximum Payoff	Taxable Case Ranking by Maximum Payoff
1 C	1 C	7 BP	7 BP
11 SC	11 SC	14 SSTR	14 SSTR
3 SS; 15 BS,BP	3 SS; 15 BS,BP	11 SC	8 BSTR
16 SS,BC	16 SS,BC	8 BSTR	11 SC
5 SSM	5 SSM	12 SP	12 SP
9 SC,BS	9 SC,BS	5 SSM	5 SSM
2 BS	2 BS	3 SS	3 SS
4 BSM	4 BSM	13 SSTR,BS	13 SSTR,BS
13 SSTR,BS	13 SSTR,BS	16 SS,BC	10 SP,BS
10 SP,BS	10 SP,BS	10 SP,BS	16 SS,BC
6 BC; 7 BP; 8 BSTR	6 BC; 7 BP; 8 BSTR	9 SC,BS	9 SC,BS
14 SSTR	14 SSTR	4 BSM	4 BSM
12 SP	12 SP	2 BS	2 BS
		1 C	1 C
		15 BS,BP	15 BS,BP
		6 BC	6 BC

Table 4A-9

Ranking of Strategies According to Minimum and Maximum Payoff, +6 Strategy Set for Nature
(cash-to-cash)

Tax-Exempt Case Ranking by Minimum Payoff	Taxable Case Ranking by Minimum Payoff	Tax-Exempt Case Ranking by Maximum Payoff	Taxable Case Ranking by Maximum Payoff
1 C	1 C	6 BC	6 BC
9 SC,BS	9 SC,BS	14 SSTR	14 SSTR
13 SSTR,BS	13 SSTR,BS	11 SC	8 BSTR
2 BS; 15 BS,BP	2 BS; 15 BS,BP	8 BSTR	4 BSM
12 SP; 16 SS,BC	10 SP,BS; 12 SP; 16 SS,BC	12 SP	10 SP,BS
10 SP,BS	4 BSM	4 BSM; 10 SP,BS	11 SC
4 BSM	3 SS	2 BS	2 BS; 12 SP
3 SS	5 SSM	13 SSTR,BS	15 BS,BP
5 SSM	6 BC; 7 BP; 8 BSTR	15 BS,BP	13 SSTR,BS
6 BC; 7 BP; 8 BSTR	11 SC	9 SC,BS	9 SC,BS
11 SC	14 SSTR	5 SSM	5 SSM
14 SSTR		3 SS	3 SS
		1 C	1 C
		16 SS,BC	16 SS,BC
		7 BP	7 BP

CHAPTER FIVE

Analysis of Some
Additional Experiments

In this chapter the solutions to some additional games are presented. The circumstances defining these games were chosen to be representative of some plausible investor's expectations concerning the payoffs that might accrue from alternative strategies and of some reasonable alternative methods of solving the game.

In one set of experiments the investor is assumed to regard the relative frequencies of past price changes as the relevant probabilities of future price movements, and then the decision problem may be treated as one of risk rather than uncertainty. In additional experiments we examine the effect of changes in the expected variance of future stock prices. In some other experiments we treat the effect of increases in the size of the option premium. Finally, in the last set of experiments we relax Assumption 5 (Section 2.2) prohibiting interim trading during the 190-day option period.

5.1
Results of Experiments Employing A Posteriori Probability Distribution

All the results reported thus far have treated the situation facing the investor as one of a game against nature. We also experimented with treating the decision problem as one of risk rather than uncertainty.

To accomplish this we estimated a set of probabilities for nature's strategies. For this purpose we employed the relative frequencies of 190-day price changes of all stocks listed on the New York Stock Exchange, initially selling between \$45 and \$55 per share, during the first half of each year from 1960 through 1964. These relative frequencies were shown in Table 3-3. The optimal strategy for an investor is that which has the highest expected utility for the calculated a posteriori probability distribution. The calculations for this case indicate which strategies would have been optimal

Table 5-1

Expected Value of the Sixteen Strategies Based on A Posteriori Probability Distribution and CMU Utility Function

Strategy	Expected Value Per Dollar of Investment 6-Month 10-Day Holding Period	
	Cash-to-Cash Case, Tax-Exempt Investor No Dividends	Cash-to-Cash Case, Taxable Investor No Dividends
1. Cash	.017	.009
2. Buy Stock	.002	.019
3. Sell Short	−.039	−.020
4. Buy Stock on Margin	−.009	.022
5. Sell Short on Margin	−.067	−.034
6. Buy Call	−.365	−.173
7. Buy Put	−.353	−.137
8. Buy Straddle	−.360	−.157
9. Sell Call, Buy Stock	.024	.025
10. Sell Put, Buy Stock	.009	.025
11. Sell Call	.051	.026
12. Sell Put	.039	.020
13. Sell Straddle, Buy Stock	.035	.031
14. Sell Straddle	.142	.071
15. Buy Stock, Buy Put	−.022	.006
16. Sell Stock, Buy Call	−.064	−.029

under alternative assumptions about utility functions during (the first halves of) the 1960–1964 period. Calculations performed for the CMU utility function are presented in Table 5-1. We find that the optimal strategy, selling Straddles, would have yielded an average

143

annual gain of approximately $28\frac{1}{2}$ per cent before taxes.[1] The corresponding optimal strategies for other utility functions are displayed in Table 4A-3.

The second column of the table presents the results of the same calculations employing the specific assumptions concerning income taxes that were described in Chapter 2. It will be noted that there is no change in the optimal strategy (selling Straddles).[2]

Not only do the calculations reported in this section show which of the strategies would have been optimal for the particular historical period considered, but they indicate how an individual would have fared in that period if he had chosen any other of our strategies. Indeed, computations of this type could be performed for any other historical period and could thus be employed for the purpose of assessing the relative merits of buying or selling options.

5.2
The Effect of Increases in the Variance
of the Distribution of Stock Prices

The experiments discussed in this section are based on the assumption that the stock price prevailing at the end of the 190-day period is a drawing from a truncated normal distribution with mean equal to the median of nature's strategies. For simplicity we shall deal here only with the extended-range case, where the standard option premium is employed and the investor is exempt from income taxes.

Since the strategies of nature are discrete and range from 20 to 80 dollars by three-dollar intervals, the probability associated with the *i*th pure strategy of nature is computed from the normal distribution as follows. Let x_i be the stock price associated with the pure

---

[1] This calculation shows the average result from a strategy of writing Straddles on every security selling between $45 and $55 per share on the first trading day of the years 1960 through 1964. They do not necessarily indicate the average returns of actual options writers during the same period, however. The distribution of price changes for stocks in which options were actually written may not be the same as that for all securities selling at approximately $50 per share.

[2] The reader will note that the expected returns from some strategies with expected values near zero actually increase with the introduction of income taxes. This results from the fact that, for some strategies, gains are taxed at favorable capital gains rates and losses are rebated at regular income tax rates. See the assumptions in Section 2.1.

strategy of nature and let $P(x_i)$ be the corresponding probability. Then

$$P(x_i) = \frac{\int_{x_i-1.5}^{x_i+1.5} e^{-y^2/2\sigma^2} \, dy}{\sum_{j=1}^{21} \int_{x_j-1.5}^{x_j+1.5} e^{-y^2/2\sigma^2} \, dy} \qquad (i = 1, \ldots, 21)$$

Values of the probability distribution given by $P(x_i)$ were computed for seventeen different values of the variance σ^2. We thus obtained seventeen different discrete distributions based on the normal distribution and differing from each other in terms of the value of the variance. For each distribution and for each of the five basic utility functions characterized by CMU, DMU (with $a = 1.6$ and 2.3) and IMU ($a = 1.6$ and 2.3) the optimal strategy was computed on the basis of the maximum expected utility criterion. The results of these computations are displayed in Table 5-2.

The configuration of optimal strategies in Table 5-2 is entirely as might be expected. For very small values of the standard deviation the optimal strategy is selling Straddles, irrespective of the utility function. For very large values of the standard deviation the optimal solution from a symmetric distribution, such as the one employed here, ought to be essentially the same as obtained from the Laplace criterion. Indeed, this is the case. The last row of Table 5-2 represents a case very similar to the Laplace criterion, since the distribution giving rise to that row has a standard deviation of 17.26. Employing the Laplace criterion implies a standard deviation of 18.1. The optimal strategies are the same with the exception of the DMU ($a = 2.3$) utility function where the Laplace criterion calls for Strategy 15, Buy Stock, Buy Put, which would, however, undoubtedly become the optimal strategy for some standard deviation greater than 17.26. For the CMU and DMU utility functions, Strategy 1, Cash, is a transitional phase between the strategies which are optimal for low values and those optimal for large values of the standard deviation. This transitional phase is small for CMU, larger for DMU with $a = 1.6$, and largest for DMU with $a = 2.3$, as might be expected. In the cases of the IMU utility functions, this phase is missing altogether, and the rational investor switches directly into buying Puts when the standard

Table 5-2

Optimal Strategies for Truncated Normal Prior Distribution of Stock Price Changes with Zero Means and Different Variances

Standard Deviation of the Computed Discrete Distribution	Utility Function				
	CMU	DMU $a = 1.6$	DMU $a = 2.3$	IMU $a = 1.6$	IMU $a = 2.3$
2.29	14 SSTR	14 SSTR	14 SSTR	14 SSTR	14 SSTR
4.33	14 SSTR	14 SSTR	14 SSTR	14 SSTR	14 SSTR
6.42	14 SSTR	14 SSTR	9 SC,BS	14 SSTR	7 BP
8.52	14 SSTR	1 C	1 C	7 BP	7 BP
10.49	11 SC	1 C	1 C	7 BP	7 BP
12.14	1 C	1 C	1 C	7 BP	7 BP
13.43	7 BP	1 C	1 C	7 BP	7 BP
14.39	7 BP	1 C	1 C	7 BP	7 BP
15.10	7 BP	1 C	1 C	7 BP	7 BP
15.65	7 BP	1 C	1 C	7 BP	7 BP
16.06	7 BP	1 C	1 C	7 BP	7 BP
16.38	7 BP	1 C	1 C	7 BP	7 BP
16.64	7 BP	1 C	1 C	7 BP	7 BP
16.84	7 BP	15 BS,BP	1 C	7 BP	7 BP
17.01	7 BP	15 BS,BP	1 C	7 BP	7 BP
17.15	7 BP	15 BS,BP	1 C	7 BP	7 BP
17.26	7 BP	8 BSTR	1 C	7 BP	7 BP

deviation increases sufficiently to make selling Straddles no longer profitable. The optimal strategies for the DMU utility function with $a = 1.6$ indicate clearly that a conservative investor should sell Straddles for a low standard deviation, move into Cash (bonds) for intermediate values of the standard deviation, assume a protected position consisting of buying the stock and buying a Put for still more volatile securities and, finally, become a buyer of Straddles for the highest level of volatility.

5.3
The Effect of Increasing the Amount of the Option Premium

Throughout the study we have assumed that the option premium was a constant percentage of the purchase price of the stock and thus independent of the expected price distribution of the underlying shares. It is well known, however, that options on volatile stocks tend to command higher premiums. Indeed, the empirical results in Section 1.4 indicate that the option premium tends to rise with increases in the volatility of past common stock prices. Therefore, for the extended-range strategy set, where the states of nature (future market prices) are enumerated over a range whose lower bound is 30 points below and whose upper bound is 30 points above the initial market price, the assumption of a fixed option premium is particularly objectionable.

We attempted to remedy this problem in the following way: Using the empirical results of Section 1.4, we could estimate how the typical option premium varied with changes in the volatility of the underlying common stock. Applying this volatility coefficient to the difference between the measured volatility of the standard-range and the extended-range case, we were able to calculate by how much the option premium could be expected to change from one case to the other. It was found that if the characteristic volatility of the underlying common stock conformed to the extended-range rather than the standard-range case, we would expect the option premium to increase by approximately $80 for a Put or Call and $160 for a Straddle. We then recalculated the extended-range case on the basis of the larger option premiums.

The results, reported for convenience in the last row of Table 4-13, were generally as expected. Option buying, the predominant optimal strategy for the extended range, became less favored as an optimal strategy, since the option premiums were greater. On the other hand, the relevant frequency of option writing as an optimal strategy was unchanged. In general, the changes in results tended to be fairly small. In many cases the optimal strategies remained unchanged. Moreover, strategies involving the sale or purchase of options still tended to predominate as optimal strategies.

5.4
The Effect of Interim Trading Within the Option Period

One objection that can be raised to the preceding analysis is that the investor is allowed to take no action whatsoever during the option period. While it may be true that most options, if they are exercised at all, are exercised only at the end of the option period (or within a few days of the expiration date of the option), still there might be certain trading strategies that option writers might wish to undertake during the option period.

Suppose, for example, that an individual wrote a Call option without owning the stock (Strategy 11). Further assume that after the option is written the stock begins to rise in price, contrary to the expectation of the option writer. It may well be that the writer would now like to cover himself by buying the shares that he expects will be needed to fulfill his option contract. In the previous analysis, however, the writer could not protect himself in this way. He was required to wait until the expiration date of the contract and then buy the shares he was required to deliver at the then current market price. It would clearly be of considerable interest to examine what the effects of relaxing this rigid prohibition against interim trading would be on our optimal strategies.

The difficulties involved in relaxing this assumption have already been mentioned.[3] Once interim trading is permitted, there are countless trading rules that could be formulated and it is difficult to generalize from the results obtained for any single rule. Nevertheless, we decided that it would be informative to consider the effects of permitting interim trading under some rather simplified conditions. Moreover, in order to increase the applicability of results, we did try to formulate a trading rule that was, in a sense, archetypical of a number of plausible interim investment strategies.

Our basic assumption was that if an investor is in a long position and sees the market price advance during his investment period, he will simply let the long position run. In the language of market traders, this embodies the popular investment nostrum "let profits run." If, on the other hand, the investor is in a long position and he sees the market price of the shares fall below his purchase price during his investment period, at some point he is assumed to liquidate his long position in order to limit his losses. In the language of the stock trader, he acts to "cut losses short."

From this very simple model of trading behavior we have

---

[3] See Chapter 2, pages 37 through 38.

formulated a specific set of interim trading rules for each of our sixteen strategies. The investor is assumed to look at the market price of the shares at the end of three months. Suppose the price is $55, five points above the initial market price. We assume that the investor then simply extrapolates the five-point rise over the next three-month period. Thus, he assumes that the price at the end of six months (i.e., approximately at the end of the option period) will be $60 per share. Thus, if the investor had sold stock short (Strategies 3 and 5), he would cover his short position at the end of three months in order to limit his losses. Similarly, if the investor had written a Call option without owning the stock (Strategy 11) he would buy stock at $55 at the end of three months, anticipating that the option would be exercised at the end of the contract period. He would calculate that buying now would save him from a greater loss later. On the other hand, all long positions remain unchanged in anticipation of even greater profits at the end of the six-month ten-day period.

The basic principle is that the investor looks at the market price of the shares at the end of three months (P_3). He then makes a prediction that the six-month price (P_6) will be $50 + 2(P_3 - 50)$. On the basis of this prediction of the six-month price, he takes covering action to limit any expected losses.[4] If, however, the six-month price will provide an even greater profit than the three-month price, he lets his profits run and liquidates his position only at the end of the option period.

One can easily see that covering action in the event of a decline in the market price of the shares would proceed in a wholly anal-

---

[4] Specifically, we assumed that the investor would take covering action if the return per dollar of investment were less, based on the estimated six-month price (P_6), than it would be if covering action were taken at price (P_3). For some of the heavily margined strategies (e.g., Strategy 14, Sell Straddle) covering action is not always taken whenever it is possible to limit the *dollar* losses from the Put or Call side of the option that is eventually exercised. It turned out, for example, that since covering the Call side of the option would entail purchasing a round lot of shares, the investor's dollar investment would be increased considerably. In such a case, the return per dollar of investment might be less if covering action were taken than if it were not taken, even though covering action would reduce the dollar loss from the Call side of the option. In other words, covering action was only taken if the return *per dollar of investment* was greater by covering at P_3 than it would be if the investor liquidated his position on the basis of P_6.

As a result of these assumptions an additional set of 42 games was solved, making the total number of experiments 1056.

ogous way. Suppose that the price falls from $50 to $45 per share at the end of three months. If the investor has a long position in the stock he will sell out at $45 in anticipation of an even greater loss at the end of the six-month holding period. Alternatively, suppose that an investor undertook the strategy of writing a Put option without owning the stock (Strategy 12). If P_3 is $45, the decision-maker will expect P_6 to be $40 and he will, therefore, anticipate that the Put option will be exercised at the end of the contract period. In this case, covering entails selling stock short. When the Put is exercised, the investor will use the shares that are put to him to liquidate his short position. If the investor's anticipation relative to P_6 is correct, this short sale will tend to reduce his losses.

For Strategy 10 (Sell Put, Buy Stock) the covering action will involve two interim transactions. In the first place, the long position in the stock must be liquidated at P_3. In addition, the stock must be sold short in anticipation of the exercise of the Put option at the end of the contract period.

It should be emphasized that in this analysis covering action is construed to mean only the undertaking of those trades which will tend to limit losses or prevent gains from eroding further. Thus if an investor undertakes Strategy 1 (Cash), he will be assumed to take no action at the end of three months irrespective of the market price that then prevails. This is so because his final profits are unaffected by market price changes. Thus the investor is not allowed to switch from cash to a long or short position, depending upon what happens to stock prices within the option period.[5] The only interim trades permitted are those that will reduce the risk exposure of the decision-maker if his expectations are correct.

Similarly, option buyers are assumed to take no covering action. Suppose a Call buyer noticed that P_3 is $55 per share, $5 over the contract price. Since he expects P_6 to be $60, he will simply hold his Call in anticipation of even greater gains at the end of the contract period. On the other hand, suppose that P_3 is $45. In this case, the option cannot be exercised at a profit. It is true that the investor also expects that the option will be worthless on its expiration date

---

[5] Nor is an investor allowed to switch from an unlevered to a levered long position if the market price has risen in the middle of the contract period.

(since P_6 is expected to be \$40), but the loss is no greater at the end of the period and no covering action is possible to limit this loss.[6]

In calculating returns per dollar of investment over the six-month ten-day holding period, we adopted the following procedure for cases where interim trading was undertaken. Whenever a position was liquidated (such as the selling out of the long position at the end of three months), the proceeds obtained were assumed to be invested in short-term securities over the remaining three months. In cases where covering entailed putting up extra dollars (such as purchasing shares to cover a Call option which previously was written by an investor who did not own the stock), the investment over the 190-day holding period was considered to be the average of the amounts invested during each of the two three-month periods. In Table 5-3 we present a list of the interim trading rules adopted for each of the 16 basic option strategies.

Thus far we have formulated a set of interim trading rules that will limit losses if the decision-maker's anticipations about subsequent movements of market prices prove correct. We call this the case of correct expectations. It is legitimate to ask, however, what would happen if the investor's expectations do not turn out to be correct. For example, suppose an investor bought stock at \$50 per share and notices that P_3 has fallen to \$45. Fearing a further decline to \$40 a share, the investor sells out at price P_3. But suppose that P_6 turns out to be, say, \$56 a share rather than \$45, the investor has suffered an actual \$5 loss by undertaking the interim trade, whereas he would have enjoyed a \$6 profit per share had he simply held on to his position until the end of the hypothesized investment period. In the language of market traders, he has been "whiplashed." In any study of interim trading, the possibility of whiplash must be con-

---

[6] Needless to say, we recognize that the interim trading rule we have introduced is itself very restrictive. In essence, it allows interim trading only at one specific time, the middle of the contract period, and trading is permitted only for the purpose of limiting losses. Of course, the price of the shares may fluctuate above and below the striking price at many times during the life of the option contract. It would be possible to formulate trading strategies for many possible interim price movements. Nevertheless, as we suggested above, no single test will ever be fully satisfactory, and it is clear that the investigation of a large number of possible interim trading strategies is not practical. At least our results should indicate the direction in which interim trading rules undertaken to limit potential losses should influence the choice of optimal strategies.

Table 5-3

**Covering Interim Trading Rules
for the Sixteen Basic Strategies**

Strategy	Price at End of 3 Months	Trading Action To Be Taken at End of 3 Months
1 Cash	$P_3 \gtreqless 50$	No action
2 Buy Stock	$P_3 \geq 50$	No action
	$P_3 < 50$	Sell out at P_3
3 Sell Short	$P_3 > 50$	Cover short position
	$P_3 \leq 50$	No action
4 Buy Stock on Margin	Same as 2.	
5 Sell Short on Margin	Same as 3.	
6 Buy Call	$P_3 \gtreqless 50$	No action
7 Buy Put	$P_3 \gtreqless 50$	No action
8 Buy Straddle	$P_3 \gtreqless 50$	No action
9 Sell Call, Buy Stock	$P_3 \geq 50$	No action
	$P_3 < 50$	Liquidate long position
10 Sell Put, Buy Stock	$P_3 \geq 50$	No action
	$P_3 < 50$	Liquidate long position and sell short
11 Sell Call	$P_3 > 50$	Buy Stock
	$P_3 \leq 50$	No action
12 Sell Put	$P_3 \geq 50$	No action
	$P_3 < 50$	Sell short
13 Sell Straddle, Buy Stock	$P_3 \geq 50$	No action
	$P_3 < 50$	Liquidate long position and sell short
14 Sell Straddle	$P_3 > 50$	Buy Stock
	$P_3 = 50$	No action
	$P_3 < 50$	Sell short
15 Buy Stock, Buy Put	$P_3 \gtreqless 50$	No action
16 Sell Short, Buy Call	$P_3 \gtreqless 50$	No action

sidered explicitly if the analysis is to be at all representative of reality.

The effect of interim trading will then be considered under two separate assumptions:

1. The case where the investor's expectations are correct.
2. The case where the investor is whiplashed.

In order to calculate the payoffs accruing to the investor for alternative prices at the end of the six-month period, correspondences had to be established between alternative values of P_6 and P_3 for the two cases. These correspondences are presented in Table 5-4. For the

Table 5-4

Correspondences Between Interim and Final Prices

---

1. Case of Correct Expectations

$$P_3 = \frac{(P_6 - 50)}{2} + 50$$

2. Whiplash Case

$$P_6 > 50, \qquad P_3 = P_6 - 11$$
$$P_6 < 50, \qquad P_3 = P_6 + 11$$
$$P_6 = 50,[1] \qquad P_3 = 50$$

---

[1] This is the only P_6 price for which no true whiplash can be defined.

case of correct expectations, P_3 is always assumed to be midway between the final price (P_6) and the striking price of the option ($50). There are, of course, any number of ways in which one can formulate the whiplash case.

The essence of the whiplash case is that the price first moves in one direction, engendering expectations of a further movement, but then moves sharply in the opposite direction. We chose to have the final price, P_6, eleven points lower or higher than P_3, depending upon whether P_3 was higher or lower than the original contract price. Thus if P_3 has risen to $56, P_6 will be assumed to be $45, eleven points from P_3, with the direction of movement opposite to that from P_0 to P_3. Once the correspondence of Table 5-4 and the interim trading rules of Table 5-3 were established, it was possible to calculate a new set of potential payoffs for alternative sets of nature facing the decision-maker.[7] It should be noted that these correspondences were set up in such a way that no value of P_3 can be inconsistent with the requirement that P_6 be between 40 and 60, which is the possible range of prices in the standard experiments.

With the new payoff matrices, we were able to calculate the investor's optimal strategies for alternative decision criteria and utility functions and for both the case of correct expectations and the whiplash case. These payoffs could then be compared with results previously obtained under the assumption that no interim trading was allowed.

It was also possible to calculate optimal strategies under the assumption that the decision-maker believes that there is some probability he will anticipate correctly the final price, but also a possibility of being whiplashed. Letting W stand for the probability weight attached to the case of correct expectations, we could form a new payoff matrix as follows:

New Payoff $= W$(payoff if expectations are correct)
$\qquad\qquad + (1 - W)$(payoff if investor is whiplashed).

Employing the matrix of new payoffs, the investor could choose his optimal strategy in the normal manner. Alternative values of W were employed ranging from $W = 1.0$ to $W = 0.0$. Comparisons with the previous results were undertaken only for the cash-to-cash case employing the 0 Strategy Set for nature.

The results of our experiments are tabulated in Tables 5-5 and 5-6. When $W = 1$, we have the case of correct expectations. We note in Table 5-5 that, relative to the standard case where no interim trading was permitted, the ability to make covering trades in the middle of the option period increases the relative frequencies with which options are written. On the other hand, the conservative strategy of buying bonds (Strategy 1, Cash) which is optimal 21.7 per cent of the time in the standard case, is no longer an optimal

---

[7] The reader should recall that a covering interim trade was not always undertaken in every instance in which it was called for in Table 5-3. We first calculated whether the return *per dollar of investment* would be improved if the covering trade were made and expectations proved correct. If the payoffs were not improved by covering, the investor was assumed to hold on to his original position.

Table 5-5

Relative Frequencies of Optimal Strategies[1]
Aggregated over All Utility Functions and Decision Criteria
for the 0 Strategy Set for Nature, Cash-to-Cash Case
(W = weight for case of correct expectations)

	Strategy	\multicolumn{7}{c	}{$W =$}	Standard Case (no interim trading)
		1.0	.9	.75	.5	.25	.1	0.0	
1	Cash			.020	.210	.273	.312	.312	.217
6	Buy Call			.001					.001
7	Buy Put	.018	.018	.020	.021	.030	.030	.030	.021
11	Sell Call	.129	.135	.129	.045	.012	.006	.006	.045
12	Sell Put	.099	.102	.090					.025
14	Sell Straddle	.753	.746	.741	.723	.684	.651	.651	.691

[1] Strategies not explicitly listed in the row headings occur with zero frequency in all cases represented by this table. Relative frequencies may not add to unity because of rounding.

strategy. In Table 5-6 it is seen that the value of the game, i.e., the expected rate of return from playing, is also increased with interim trading, when the investor's expectations turn out to be correct.

It is worth noting that the levered strategies of selling options without owning stock are especially favored when interim trading is permitted. This is so because interim trading allows the investor to protect himself from the very large unfavorable outcomes which are possible in some of the levered strategies.

Let us consider next the case where the investor is always whiplashed (i.e., the case where $W = 0$). Here we find, not surprisingly, that Strategy 1, Cash, is more frequently an optimal strategy. Moreover, as is shown in Table 5-6, the value of the game decreases in several instances.[8] In these cases the investor would have been better off not to have undertaken any interim trading at all.

Perhaps the most realistic cases are those between the two extremes. If the probability of whiplash is 0.5, we find that the investor's

[8] The value of the game stays the same only in cases where Strategy 1, Cash, was optimal in the first place.

Table 5-6

**Comparison of Value of Game With
and Without Interim Trading**
(W = weight for case of correct expectations)

Decision Criterion	$W =$							Standard Case (no interim trading)
	1.0	.9	.75	.5	.25	.1	0.0	
Minimax, CMU	.225	.155	.050	.017	.017	.017	.017	.017
Laplace, CMU	.596	.573	.538	.480	.422	.387	.364	.511
Minimax, DMU	.271	.172	.029	.029	.029	.029	.029	.029
Laplace, DMU	.645	.612	.555	.436	.273	.145	.044	.488
Minimax, IMU	.125	.089	.043	.006	.006	.006	.006	.064
Laplace, IMU	.631	.622	.609	.592	.579	.573	.569	.603

optimal strategies are about the same as for the standard case but that the value of the game tends to be slightly lower. For a value of $W = 0.75$ (i.e., the probability of the investor's expectations being correct is three-quarters), the value of the game is slightly higher than for the standard case, and writing options is more frequently an optimal strategy. This analysis suggests that unless the investor believes he has more than an equal chance of predicting the final price, given the value of P_3, he would do well not to undertake any interim trades in an attempt to limit his losses.

For investors who do not believe they are able to predict final prices from interim prices with great certainty, and hence refrain from interim trading, the results of the previous sections remain applicable.

CHAPTER SIX

Summary and Conclusions

The earlier chapters were devoted to a systematic exposition of our approach to the determination of optimal strategies in securities markets and to a detailed analysis of the solutions of numerous games against nature. It seems desirable to summarize the most significant aspects of our analysis and to discuss the results of the study and their practical implications. Section 6.1 is a review of the basic characteristics of the study. Section 6.2 contains some specific conclusions concerning optimal strategies for certain widely prevalent types of investors. Section 6.3 presents some general conclusions derived from the analysis as well as a discussion of the practical consequences of our findings for the option market.

6.1
Review of the Analytic Approach

Previous studies of the profitability of the buying or selling of securities or options on securities have characteristically based their arguments on the expected gain to be made from the security in question. In the simplest terms, if the expected gain computed on the basis of some expectations or assumptions about the probability of future security prices exceeds the cost of the security, one concludes that its purchase is profitable.

The fundamental point of departure for our study is the contention that one cannot determine the investor's most desirable course of action by considering each possible action in isolation from others.

Since the investor can, at any one time, undertake a number of different acts (buy or sell stock, buy or sell options, etc.), we must determine what is a rational strategy for him when he is confronted with an entire menu of choices. Our second major contention is that, in addition to considering the effect on rational behavior of the more or less traditional assumptions about future security prices, we must also consider the possibility that the investor cannot specify any probability distribution over prices prevailing in the future. The complete ignorance of the investor, which we are willing to assume, transforms the general problem of finding rational strategies into the specific problem of solving games against nature.

Given our basic methodological decision to treat the determination of rational strategies as a matter of solving games against nature, it became necessary (1) to define rather precisely what a game against nature consists of and (2) to endow the definition with enough flexibility so that a large variety of more or less reasonable circumstances may be characterized as games against nature. The former was accomplished by defining and enumerating the actions or pure strategies available to the investor (purchases or sales of the security, options of various sorts) and those available to nature (prices prevailing in the market at the horizon). The latter was accomplished by permitting games to differ from each other in a number of respects such as:

1. The initial and final position (cash or stock) of the investor.
2. The tax status of the investor.
3. The payment of cash dividends on the stock that is bought, sold, or optioned.
4. The size of option premiums.
5. The range of prices potentially prevailing in the market.
6. The investor's attitude toward risk as reflected by the shape of his utility function.
7. The method (decision criterion) employed by the investor for solving the game against nature.
8. The presence or absence of interim trading during the option period.

The variation in these and other aspects of the game allowed us to solve and examine the solutions of a large number of different games. Comparisons of these solutions permitted us to derive conclusions concerning the optimal strategies that may hold for a variety of investors and circumstances. Some of these are reviewed in the next two sections.

6.2
Suggested Strategies for Certain Investors

One of the purposes of our experiments was to employ the results in the formulation of optimal strategies for certain types of actual investors. Tables 6-1, 6-2, and 6-3 summarize the optimal strategies for some plausible sets of circumstances defining the decision situation. These circumstances may, with some justification, be taken to represent the actual decision situations of some investors. Specifically, it is not unreasonable to assume that some institutional investors may be accurately described by the stock-to-stock case. These institutions consistently hold an equity portfolio (or a portfolio of stocks and bonds) regardless of market conditions. Many of these institutions are also exempt from federal income taxes as, for example, college and university endowment funds and pension funds. Since such institutions are typically assumed to be risk-averse, the DMU utility function would appear to be the most applicable utility function. It is interesting to ask what the optimal strategies would be for such an institution for various alternative expectations regarding future stock-price movements.

Table 6-1 presents the average solutions for such an institutional investor for two alternative strategy sets for nature. If such a risk-averse, tax-exempt institution (holding a stock portfolio) believes that the market will rise, all optimal strategies (aggregated over all decision criteria) involve the selling of options. Over three-quarters of these optimal strategies involve buying stocks and selling options. If the institution is taxable (at a corporate income tax rate) almost 60 per cent of the optimal strategies involve the writing of options and the buying of stock, while the purchase of Call options is optimal almost 17 per cent of the time.[1]

---

[1] We have discussed in Section 4.4.2 the reasons for the changes in optimal strategies that result from the imposition of income taxes.

Table 6-1

**Relative Frequencies of Optimal Strategies
for Selected Circumstances**[1]
(stock-to-stock case; DMU utility function; $a = 2.3^2$)

	Taxable Investor		Tax-Exempt Investor	
+6 Strategy Set	6 BC	.167	9 SC,BS	.165
for Nature	9 SC,BS	.313	10 SP,BS	.341
	10 SP,BS	.099	11 SC	.002
	12 SP	.233	12 SP	.236
	13 SSTR,BS	.167	13 SSTR,BS	.257
	14 SSTR	.021		
0 Strategy Set	1 C	.451	1 C	.333
for Nature	11 SC	.049	9 SC, BS	.123
	14 SSTR	.500	11 SC	.042
			14 SSTR	.501

[1] Aggregated over all decision criteria.
[2] The number 2.3 refers to the value of the parameter a in equations (3.2) and (3.3).

In the case of the 0 Strategy Set (that is, when the institution does not expect, on average, any change in market prices) the optimal strategies for such a risk-averse investor are mainly the holding of cash (that is, buying bonds) and the selling of Straddles. We conclude that institutional investors should seriously consider writing options as an adjunct to their regular investment activities. Particularly, tax-exempt financial institutions should find that writing options against their portfolio (that is, the combination of option selling and stock buying) should increase their investment yields substantially.

Table 6-2 presents the average solutions for a cash-to-cash investor with a Composite IMU utility function. The reader will recall from Section 3.1 that the Composite IMU utility function has the following properties: the investor is assumed to be a risk averter with respect to losses, but a risk lover with respect to gains. This would appear to be a reasonable utility function for many individual investors, and it is much like the cubic utility function that has the desirable theoretical properties described in Section 3.1. The solutions in Table 6-2 may therefore offer guidance to many individual investors.

Table 6-2

**Relative Frequencies of Optimal Strategies
for Selected Circumstances[1]**
(cash-to-cash case; Composite IMU utility function $a = 2.3$)

	Taxable Investor		Tax-Exempt Investor	
+6 Strategy Set	6 BC	.814	6 BC	.593
for Nature	12 SP	.048	13 SSTR,BS	.162
	14 SSTR	.138	14 SSTR	.245
0 Strategy Set	4 BSM	.114	1 C	.167
for Nature	7 BP	.075	7 BP	.034
	11 SC	.048	14 SSTR	.799
	14 SSTR	.763		

[1] Aggregated over all decision criteria.

The table indicates that for a taxable investor who expects the market to rise (that is, who assumes that the +6 Strategy Set for nature is applicable), Call buying is the optimal strategy over 80 per cent of the time. If the investor is tax exempt and expects the market to rise, the table suggests that he should do less Call buying and do a significant amount (over 40 per cent) of Straddle selling. If the individual investor expects no change on average in market prices, Straddle selling is overwhelmingly the optimal strategy. In more than 75 per cent of the individual experiments that make up the table, the investor is advised to sell Straddles without owning the stock.[2]

Table 6-3 presents results for an investor who employs the maximum expected utility criterion based on the posterior stock price distribution. The reader will recall that this distribution was calculated by taking the 190-day price changes for all stocks on the New York Stock Exchange selling at between $45 and $55 per share on the first trading day of years 1960 through 1964. The table indicates that

---

[2] Many option dealers have argued that Straddle sellers should own the stock on which the Straddle is written. This is undesirable, however, for the 0 Strategy Set for nature as may be seen from Figure 2-5 on page 54. While selling Straddles without the stock is a more levered strategy, the Straddle seller who owns the stock is also somewhat levered because of the double jeopardy from falling prices. A declining market will lead to a double loss, one loss on the long position and the second on the Put position.

Table 6-3

Optimal Strategies for Investor Who
Employs the Maximum Expected Utility Criterion
Based on the A Posteriori Distribution

	DMU Utility Function	CMU Utility Function	IMU Utility Function	Composite IMU Utility Function
Tax-Exempt Investor Standard Premium	1 C	14 SSTR	7 BP	7 BP
Taxable Investor Standard Premium	9 BS,SC	14 SSTR	7 BP	7 BP
Tax-Exempt Investor Nonstandard Premium	9 BS,SC	14 SSTR	7 BP	7 BP

for a risk-averse taxable individual, and for a tax-exempt individual where a nonstandard (higher) option premium is received, the optimal strategy is that of buying stock and selling Call options. If the investor is neutral with respect to risk (he has a CMU utility function), the optimal strategy involves the selling of Straddles. For a risk lover (IMU utility function), the optimal strategy involves the buying of options.[3] Again, we see the critical dependence of the optimal solution on the investor's attitude toward risk.

6.3
General Conclusions

We conclude with the following broad observations:

1. Formulating the individual's choice of action in the securities option market as a game against nature yields sensible results and is theoretically satisfying.

---

[3] Put rather than Call options are optimal because (1) they are cheaper, and (2) the a posteriori distribution of stock price changes over the first halves of 1960 through 1964 includes the very sharp market decline of 1962. We warn the reader, however, that this distribution may not be representative of more recent distributions, nor of distributions formed over longer periods of time. Moreover, the distribution of price changes for all $50 stocks may not be the same as that for stocks on which options have been written.

2. The manner in which optimal strategies depend on utility functions, tax assumptions, decision criteria, and the expected price range is intuitively plausible.
3. Fully satisfactory intuitive explanations are difficult to provide for each experiment since they depend on more or less inexact terms such as "long" or "short" positions, and "leverage," whereas the actual answer depends upon precise numerical magnitudes.
4. Nevertheless, the use of stock options by both buyers and sellers appears to be wholly rational; indeed, it would seem that many more investors could profitably employ option strategies.

Perhaps the most remarkable result of our study is the extent to which strategies involving the use of options, especially option writing, predominate over other possible stock market strategies. Even when the optimal strategy involves the purchase of stock, the investor is almost always advised to combine his purchase with the writing of options. This result holds for all investor attitudes toward risk, with every decision criterion employed, and over all distribution of stock price changes. Whatever conditions we assume for the game against nature, it is impossible to escape the conclusion that option strategies are desirable, even when, as is the case throughout these experiments, the payoffs include all transaction costs, including actual brokerage charges and dealer spreads between the premiums received and premiums paid for stock options.

In view of the general conclusion of our study that option dealing is not only perfectly rational but also a very desirable strategy for most investors, the natural question arises. Why are options used so little in practice?

As was mentioned in Chapter 1, option transactions have increased considerably in recent years. Nevertheless, it was indicated in Table 1-1 that the ratio of total option volume to total volume of the New York Stock Exchange declined slightly between 1960 and 1968. Thus, in relative terms, option dealing appears to have declined, at least until 1968. In view of our conclusions about the rationality of option strategies, it is important to explain the relatively small size of the option market.

We believe there are three major reasons for this state of affairs. The first is the lack of education about options among the investing public. The second concerns the traditional and legal constraints against option dealing for many institutions. The last reason is the disorganized state of the market. We shall deal with each of these arguments in turn.

It is a fact of life that, despite an increase in recent interest in the market, the mechanics of dealing in stock options are relatively unknown, not only to the general public but also to professional investment managers. Moreover, even if some individuals are aware of the possibility of buying options, few investors have any understanding of the method by which options may be sold. Perhaps the biggest roadblock in the way of the growth of the market is the lack of information about it.

Second, many investing institutions, particularly some tax-exempt institutions, for whom the writing of options is most likely to be an optimal strategy, are prevented from entering the market by legal and traditional restrictions. Chapter 1 mentioned that options have had a rather unsavory history. The bad name that they have acquired is largely responsible for many of the traditional taboos against option trading. In addition, option contracts are regarded in some states as gambling contracts, with the result that many institutions within those states are legally prevented from writing options. Furthermore, the short-term nature of stock options and the short-term trading that is often required by their use (as, for example, when the Put half of a Straddle is exercised and the Put shares are then disposed of) have led many institutional investors to think that option writing was unsuited to their general mode of operation.

Another reason that tax-exempt institutions have not engaged in widespread option selling is the attitude of the Internal Revenue Service toward this practice. The difficulty stems from the fact that the premiums from unexercised Call or Put options constitute ordinary income. The Internal Revenue Service has construed such income to be "unrelated business income," which would be taxable income to an otherwise tax-exempt institution.[4] The November 1966

---

[4] See Revenue Ruling 66–47, *Cumulative Bulletin:* Internal Revenue Service, Vol. 1966-1, pp. 149–151.

legislation, described in Chapter 2, presumably removes the problem insofar as Straddles are concerned. Congress ruled that the premium from the unexpired part of a Straddle constitutes a short-term capital gain rather than income. Thus, it would appear that tax considerations should not prevent a tax-exempt institution from writing Straddles. However, there is still a difficulty regarding the tax implications involved in writing ordinary Call or Put options, and some tax-exempt institutions are still reluctant to deal even in Straddles without a clearer idea of IRS policy.

The final factor holding back the development of the option market is its relatively inefficient organization. The process of getting an option buyer and seller together is currently inefficient and cumbersome. There is no central marketplace. With the exception of Goodbody & Co. (see pp. 16–17), the option firms that serve as middlemen usually try to match individual buy orders with individual sellers and do not make continuous markets. If an option on an inactively traded security is demanded, the middleman may at times be unable to find an option writer who is willing to sell options on that particular security. Even if the option firm is successful in arranging the trade, the procedure may have involved as many as fifteen telephone calls to potential writers. In addition, there is no systematic reporting of either actual option trades or of offers to buy and sell, except on a limited number of actively traded issues. Thus it is extremely difficult for either a buyer or a seller to know what a fair market price is or whether there are any participants on the other side of the market. In view of the cumbersomeness of the operation and the lack of detailed reporting on option trades, bids, and offers, it is not surprising that many investors have refused to deal in options.

This discussion suggests that the future development of the option market will be influenced significantly by the extent to which the organization of the market is improved. We believe that there are two principal requisites for any significant improvement. The first is the establishment of a central marketplace where all bids and offers may be cleared; the second is the development of a plan for the reporting of firm bids and offers as well as actual trades to all market participants. The rather informal ad hoc nature of the present arrangements appears to be the major obstacle in the way of further development of the option market.[5]

One final suggestion that may be of enormous help in encouraging the development of the market is that option contracts be made more homogeneous. Such homogeneity would appear necessary for the establishment of a secondary market in option contracts in which both option writers and buyers could sell their respective obligations and rights before the expiration date of the contract. At the present time, practically each individual option contract that is written is different. For example, on January 2, 190-day options may be written on Ford at striking prices of 50, $50\frac{1}{8}$, and $50\frac{1}{4}$. On January 3, 190-day options may be written at the same three prices, but the expiration date will be July 12 rather than July 11. Thus all six contracts differ with respect to their terms despite their general similarity. Clearly, no effective secondary market can be established with such a heterogeneous group of contracts.

Consider the alternative that all option contracts written during the month of January with a duration of between six and seven months be written with a maturity date of August 1. Then all such option contracts written during January would expire on the same day. Moreover, the contract prices themselves could be standardized by requiring that the contract price of an option would always be the market price *rounded* to the nearest dollar. In this case all six of the sample contracts discussed in the previous paragraph would be homogeneous and there would be some hope of establishing an effective secondary market. Option contracts could thus be made

---

[5] A newly organized firm, Market Monitor Data Inc., plans to begin a computer service to store all offers to write options and all bids to purchase them. Brokers could then utilize the computer to ascertain what options are being offered or sought on any stock. Should such an all-inclusive reporting service be established, we believe the development of the market would accelerate. See "Puts and Calls," *Wall Street Journal,* February 12, 1968.

In a more ambitious and potentially much more significant undertaking, the Chicago Board of Trade initiated a study in early 1967 to determine the feasibility of establishing a central marketplace for options. In this market, initial contracts could be negotiated and both option buyers and option writers could reenter the market to sell their claims or cover their obligations. See Jonathan R. Laing, "Chicago Board of Trade Plans To Set Up Market in Put and Call Stock Options," *Wall Street Journal,* Feb. 19, 1969.

analogous to futures contracts in commodities where effective trading markets do exist.

In conclusion, we believe that option trading is wholly rational and that many individuals and institutions who do not now deal in this market would find it profitable to do so. Whether or not the market will in fact grow to the size we think is justified will depend in large part on improvement in its organization. Ideally all bids and offers for options should be cleared in a central marketplace, and secondary markets in options with full public reporting might then also be established. Of course, this will be an enormous task that will require the ingenuity and imagination of the best minds in the business and the willingness to discard the present inefficient organization.

Bibliography

Ayres, Herbert F., "Risk Aversions in the Warrant Markets." *Industrial Management Review* 5 (Fall 1963): 45–53.

Bachelier, Louis, "Theory of Speculation." In Cootner, Paul H., ed. *The Random Character of Stock Market Prices*. Cambridge: M.I.T. Press, 1964: 17–75.

Baumol, W. J., Malkiel, B. G., and Quandt, R. E. "The Valuation of Convertible Securities." *Quarterly Journal of Economics* 80 (February 1966): 48–59.

Boness, A. James. "Elements of a Theory of Stock-Option Value." *Journal of Political Economy* 72 (April 1964): 163–175.

———, "Some Evidence on the Profitability of Trading in Put and Call Options." In Cootner, Paul H., ed. *The Random Character of Stock Market Prices*: 475–496.

Clews, Henry. *Twenty-Eight Years in Wall Street*. New York: Irving Publishing Co., 1888.

Commerce Clearing House. *U.S. Master Tax Guide*. New York, 1968.

Cootner, Paul H., ed. *The Random Character of Stock Market Prices*. Cambridge: M.I.T. Press, 1964.

Cowing, C. B. *Populists, Plungers, and Progressives*. Princeton: Princeton University Press, 1965.

Cragg, John G., and Malkiel, Burton G. "The Consensus and Accuracy of Some Predictions of the Growth of Corporate Earnings." *Journal of Finance* 23 (March 1968): 67–84.

Cunnion, John D. *How To Get Maximum Leverage from Puts and Calls*. Larchmont, N.Y.: Business Reports, Inc., 1966.

Davis, Joseph S. *Essays in the Earlier History of American Corporations*. Cambridge: Harvard University Press, 1917.

Duguid, Charles. *The Story of the Stock Exchange*. London: Grant Richards, 1901.

Emery, Henry C. "Speculation on the Stock and Produce Exchanges of the

United States." In *Studies in History, Economics and Public Law,* VII. New York: Columbia University, 1896: 285–512.

Fama, Eugene F. "Mandelbrot and the Stable Paretian Hypothesis." *Journal of Business* 36 (October 1963): 420–429.

Filer, Herbert. *Understanding Put and Call Options.* New York: Crown Publishers, 1959.

Franklin, C. B., and Colberg, M. R. "Puts and Calls — A Factual Survey." *Journal of Finance* (March 1958): 21–34.

Friedman, Milton, and Savage, Leonard J. "The Utility Analysis of Choices Involving Risk." *Journal of Political Economy* 56 (August 1948): 279–304.

Gup, Benton E. "The Economics of the Security Option Markets." Ph.D. dissertation, University of Cincinnati, 1966.

Harbaugh, A. W. "Expected Value of Options, Warrants and Convertible Securities." Paper presented at the 27th National Meeting of the Operations Research Society of America, Boston, May 1965.

Hesslein, Max. "Puts and Calls." Memorandum presented to the SEC, Washington, 1934.

Katz, Richard. "The Profitability of Put and Call Option Writing." *Industrial Management Review* 5 (Fall 1963): 55–69.

Klevorick, Alvin K. "Capital Budgeting under Risk: A Mathematical-Programming Approach." Econometric Research Program, Research Memorandum No. 89, Princeton University, September 1967.

Krefetz, G., and Marrossi, R. *Investing Abroad.* New York: Harper and Row, 1965.

Kruizenga, Richard J. "An Introduction to the Option Contract." In Cootner, Paul H., ed. *The Random Character of Stock Market Prices:* 377–391.

———, "Profit Returns from Purchasing Puts and Calls," in Cootner, Paul H., ed. *The Random Character of Stock Market Prices:* 392–411.

Laing, Jonathan R., "Chicago Board of Trade Plans To Set Up Market in Put and Call Stock Options." *Wall Street Journal,* February 19, 1969.

Lederman, David. "Put and Call Options with Special Emphasis on Option Portfolios." Dissertation submitted to the Graduate School of Business of Stanford University, 1969.

Luce, R. Duncan, and Raiffa, Howard. *Games and Decisions.* New York: Wiley, 1957: 275–326.

Mandelbrot, Benoit. "The Variation of Certain Speculative Markets." *Journal of Business* 36 (October 1963): 394–419.

Markowitz, Harry. *Portfolio Selection.* New York: Wiley, 1959.

———, "The Utility of Wealth." *Journal of Political Economy* 60 (April 1952): 151–158.

Milnor, John. "Games against Nature." In Thrall, R. M., Coombs, C. W., and Davis, R. L. *Decision Processes.* New York: Wiley, 1954: 49–59.

Pratt, John W. "Risk Aversion in the Small and in the Large." *Econometrica* 32 (January–April 1964): 122–136.

"Puts and Calls." *Wall Street Journal,* February 12, 1968.

BIBLIOGRAPHY

Reinach, Anthony M. *The Nature of Puts and Calls.* New York: The Book-mailer, 1961.

Rosett, Richard. "Estimating the Utility of Wealth from Call Option Trans-actions." In Hester, Donald, and Tobin, James. *Risk Aversion and Port-folio Choice.* New York: Wiley, 1967: 154–169.

Samuelson, Paul A. "Rational Theory of Warrant Pricing." *Industrial Manage-ment Review* 6 (Spring 1965): 13–32.

Schneider, Hermann, and Wintrub, Warren. *Tax Savings Opportunities in Securities Transactions.* New York: Lybrand, Ross Brothers and Mont-gomery, 1966.

Securities and Exchange Commission. *Report on Put and Call Options.* Wash-ington: U.S. Government Printing Office, 1961.

Sprenkle, Case M. "Warrant Prices as Indicators of Expectations and Prefer-ences." *Yale Economic Essays,* Vol. 1, No. 2 (1961): 178–231.

The Twentieth Century Fund. *The Security Markets.* New York, 1935.

Thomas, W. A., and Morgan, E. V. *The Stock Exchange.* London: Elek Books, 1962.

U.S. Congress, Senate, Senate Report 1455. *Stock Exchange Practices.* 73d Cong., 2d sess., 1934.

U.S. Internal Revenue Service. 1954 Internal Revenue Code: Section 210(c), (1); Section 1234(a) and (b).

Index